Count

~

TENNESSEE

A Guide Book
from Country Roads Press

Country Roads
~ of ~
TENNESSEE

Fronda Throckmorton

Illustrated by
Victoria Sheridan

With a Foreword by Chet Atkins

Country Roads Press
CASTINE • MAINE

Country Roads of Tennessee

Published by Country Roads Press
P.O. Box 286, Lower Main Street
Castine, Maine 04421

Text and cover design by Edith Allard.
Illustrations by Victoria Sheridan.
Typesetting by Camden Type 'n Graphics.

ISBN 1–56626–041–8

Library of Congress Cataloging-in-Publication Data

Throckmorton, Fronda, 1961–
    Country roads of Tennessee / Fronda Throckmorton ;
illustrations, Victoria Sheridan.
        p.   cm.
    Includes index.
    ISBN 1-56626-041-8 : $9.95
    1. Tennessee—Guidebooks.   2. Automobile travel—
Tennessee—Guidebooks.   I. Title.
    F434.3.T48   1994
    917.6804'53–dc20   93–44334
                                                            CIP

Printed in the United States of America.
10 9 8 7 6 5 4 3 2 1

For my husband, Rob.
I love you.

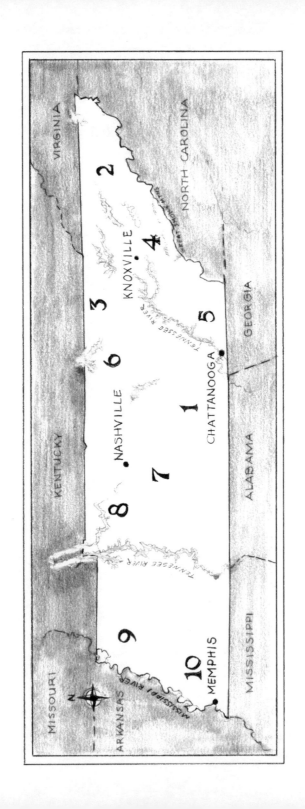

Contents

(& Key to Tennessee Country Roads)

Foreword

When you talk about Tennessee, you're talking about a place pretty close to my heart.

My paternal great-grandfather came to East Tennessee from Virginia in the late 1700s. I don't know much about him, but there is a pretty good history of my grandfather. He lived in Union County about twenty miles north of Knoxville and was a cabinetmaker and a farmer.

A champion fiddler, my grandfather also made fiddles for most of his nine children. He was an ardent supporter of President Abraham Lincoln and the North during the Civil War, which was not unusual in that part of Tennessee.

I was born and raised in the same dirt-poor Clinch Mountains in a holler between Corryton and Luttrell, about a quarter of a mile from the Southern Railroad line. We raised tobacco, turnips, beans, corn, and potatoes, and we had a nice plum and apple orchard.

I must say that for the first eleven years of my life, I was very unhappy in East Tennessee. I was sick with asthma and we were very poor—so poor that I remember having sores from malnutrition. But everyone else was in the same boat. Those were the lean years, not only for us, but for the whole country.

By the time I was eighteen, I was in the music business. I was fired from jobs in Denver, Cincinnati, Richmond, and other cities.

Foreword

When I returned to Tennessee, by way of Nashville, the pieces of the puzzle finally started fitting together. Nashvillians took me into their hearts. For years I have wanted to buy billboards all across the state saying, "Thanks Tennessee." I've traveled the world over, but I'm glad I come home to Tennessee. It has so many treasures, from the mountains to the Mississippi Delta. And I guess its greatest natural resource would be the people, don't you know. There are no better on earth.

Country Roads of Tennessee includes what I love about the state—the places, the people, the food, and the rich history. Everything from which meat-and-three has the best biscuits to where you can find homemade Amish molasses to go with them. Fronda Throckmorton has painted a vivid picture of Tennessee—the state we're both proud to call home.

Chet Atkins, C.G.P.

Introduction

On a cold November night, my husband and I spent hours searching for the trailhead to Charit Creek, a rustic lodging cabin in Big South Fork National River and Recreation Area. Anxious and hungry, Rob and I finally found the parking lot and put on our gear for the almost two-mile hike.

With the aid of only one flashlight, we stumbled in the dark over branches and dips in the trail, furiously rubbing our gloved hands together to keep warm in the twenty-degree winds that whipped around us. Unsure of where we were going and sure that we had missed dinner, Rob and I weren't in the best of spirits.

Seeing lamplight in the clearing and hearing voices in the cabins, we trudged toward the signs of life and were met by resident manager Scott Barker and his wife, Kim. They invited us to share some of their homemade chili and corn bread—not the dinner they served the rest of the guests, but some of their *own* food. "Go ahead, we made extra," they said. "We're sorry you missed dinner."

That single incident typifies our experience of traveling across our home state of Tennessee—people opening their homes, their businesses, their lives to strangers.

From the mountains of East Tennessee to the flatlands of West Tennessee, we've met some of the most genuinely good people. Interesting folks, such as Ned Lathrop, a Wisconsin native who moved to Memphis just to "be near Elvis." Or Judd Brown, who stayed an hour after closing time at the

American Museum of Science and Energy, sharing with us his memories of Oak Ridge and growing up in the "Secret City." And then there's H. B. and Mildred Plummer, an adorable elderly couple who own a grocery and old museum outside of Clarksville. We talked about everything, from their tomato plants to the party their grandchildren and children were hosting for Mrs. Plummer's birthday the following day.

That's what traveling Tennessee's country roads is all about—connecting with people, learning the history of various areas, and seeing places you may never have heard of. In our travels, my husband and I have found some real Tennessee treasures, such as a restaurant in Coker Creek that serves *the best* fried chicken; the Clarksville Montgomery County Museum, a fantastic small museum of history; the Spit and Whittle Gang, a group of mostly retired men who whittle away the hours in the shade of the Macon County Courthouse; and the Dale Hollow National Fish Hatchery, an entertaining look at trout raising.

Tennessee's history is fascinating, from the creation of the State of Franklin to the tragic Trail of Tears to the Civil War battle sites. More Civil War battles were fought on our soil than in any other state except Virginia. And we've produced some exceptional leaders, including three U.S. presidents.

Our musical roots grow deep—from the birthplace of the blues in Memphis to the musical heritage of the people of the Appalachian Mountains to the country music of Nashville.

Country Roads of Tennessee covers a little bit of everything—small towns, music, history, nature, and people. This book is not all-inclusive—there's much more to see in Tennessee. You can take these trips or use them to plan your own route along our beautiful country roads.

I want to thank all the gracious people who provided information for this book, from the chambers of commerce to the historical societies to the people we stopped on the street. In many ways, this has been a joint venture—with me writing and my husband driving, taking visual notes and remaining patient every time I said, "Hey, was that a historical marker? We better go look at it."

Tennessee's a great place. We hope you enjoy it, too.

To help clarify road designations, I've used the following abbreviations: I = interstate, US = US route or highway, State = state route or highway, and County = county road.

1 ~

Lynchburg

to

Chattanooga

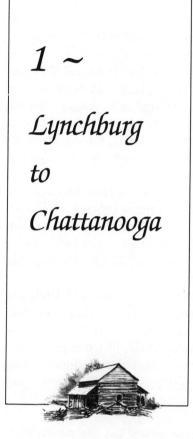

From Nashville, take I-24 east to Manchester (State 55). Go twenty-five miles south through Tullahoma to Lynchburg. (In Tullahoma, State 55 runs north with US 41A before State 55 splits off to the south again.) The total trip length from Lynchburg to Chattanooga is 110 miles.

Highlights: *The Jack Daniel Distillery, the enticing campus of the University of the South, the sights and smells of the Dutch Maid Bakery, the Victorian village of the Monteagle Sunday School Assembly, a breathtaking ride on the Lookout Mountain Incline Railway, the hot history of the Coke Ovens National Historic Site in Dunlap, the water animals of the Tennessee Aquarium, and the history of the Hunter Museum of Art in Chattanooga.*

Welcome to Lynchburg, population 361. Chartered in 1833, the town was first settled around 1800. Plenty of homes were built here, but one of the original buildings still standing is the Bobo House, built in 1812. Lynchburg is the county seat of Moore County, named for Gen. William Moore, an early settler in the area.

The beautiful Moore County Courthouse serves as the centerpiece of the town; it was constructed in 1885 by Lynchburg citizens who also made the bricks. Men appointed to oversee the construction reported on April 6, 1885, that the work was well done, and congratulated the county "upon having the neatest, most convenient, and with all, the *cheapest* courthouse in the state."

The "downtown" square is lined with several old interesting businesses. At the Lynchburg Ladies' Handiwork, you can watch women sewing, quilting, and creating. Several women cleaned up the formerly abandoned store in 1970 to have a place to showcase their work. Today, the store features fabric lampshades, old-fashioned sunbonnets, afghans, stuffed toys, and cornhusk dolls.

On the opposite side of the square is The Iron Kettle, an old-time eatery offering Tennessee home cooking. Their specialty is "whiskey whoppers." Fired on the grill, the fresh hamburger patty is splashed with whiskey just before being ensconced between buns. Try it—you'll like it with that little extra bite.

Miss Mary Bobo's Boarding House, an 1866 landmark famous for its country ham, redeye gravy, and hot buttermilk biscuits, is just down the road. Miss Mary Bobo ran the restaurant and the boardinghouse from 1908 until her death in 1983. The house still continues Miss Bobo's tradition of a big southern-style midday meal. Seating is limited, however, and waiting lists are long. We couldn't get in, but maybe you'll have better luck.

Just a short walk from the square lies the reason most people come to this little town—the Jack Daniel Distillery. America's oldest distillery, it was the first one to be registered with the U.S. government. "Uncle Jack," as he's fondly referred to, registered the distillery with Uncle Sam in 1866 when he was sixteen. Its "Number One" designation is the reason the distillery is on the National Register of Historic Places today.

Jasper Newton (Jack) Daniel was a mere fourteen when he bought the still for twenty-five dollars from a Lutheran minister whose parish didn't take too kindly to the preacher makin' moonshine on the side. The preacher went straight

Visit the Jack Daniel Distillery

and sold the still to Daniel, who then settled here next to a cave with naturally flowing, almost completely iron-free, cold springwater—the kind you apparently need for good whiskey.

Some 250,000 people visit the forty-five-building distillery each year. The free tour starts in an old paneled room filled with stacks of previously used sour mash whiskey barrels. Take a poker chip and wait for the color of your chip to be called. The one-hour tour includes a little more than a mile of walking and a lot of stairs, so wear comfortable shoes.

The first stop is a room with long wooden benches where you watch a film about how Daniel's whiskey is made. Besides using the springwater, Daniel bought only the best grain and then used a charcoal mellowing process to make it Tennessee sour mash and not bourbon whiskey.

The rest of the tour includes seven-story warehouses filled with fifty-five-gallon white oak barrels of aging whiskey; the sawmill area, where sugar maple trees are burned to make the charcoal; the cave with fifty-six-degree springwater; an Italian marble statue of the former five-foot-two-inch Daniel; a room where you can see the charcoal vat process and inhale a whiff of pretty strong stuff; Daniel's original office with a potbelly stove, a safe, and an old wooden desk cluttered with worn ledgers; and the fermenting room, with gray metal vats about twenty feet in diameter filled with bubbling, mustard yellow gunk—otherwise known as the mash.

The tour ends in a saloon complete with wooden tables and stools and the original mirror that Daniel used in his saloon, The White Rabbit. After having been teased for an hour with the warm aroma of liquor, you get to belly up to the bar and order a . . . *lemonade.* Liquor isn't served or sold here— Moore County has been dry since 1909. It just goes to show, though, that the chase is usually more fun than the catch.

Take State 55 south out of Lynchburg, then take State 50 east to Winchester. Roll down the windows and take in the scents and sounds of these country roads. During the summer, the crickets and birds are singing and the farms are full of freshly cut hay. Sunlight dances through the slats of old gray barns, and the fields are green as far as the eye can see.

Winchester, the county seat of Franklin County, is one of the state's oldest settlements, founded by the winners of the West when they crossed the Appalachians. Named in honor of Benjamin Franklin, the county was first settled in 1800. Franklin County was also supposedly the only county to vote to secede from the state of Tennessee in 1861, but Tennessee's secession from the Union in 1861 made it unnecessary.

Pay a visit to the original county jail, located on First Avenue NE. The Old Jail Museum used to hold the dregs of society, but now it features the cream of the county, with exhibits on pioneer relics, Cherokee artifacts, and Civil War bits of history from the skirmishes that occurred in the area. Built in 1897 and used until 1972, the county jail held a maximum of sixteen prisoners. It closed because of overcrowding, explains Ruth McNutt, a hostess for the museum, which is open from mid-March to mid-November. "At this time in the country, every city had its own jail," she says. "But around 1969, they closed all of the city jails and started using just the county jails. So this became a museum in 1973."

A tour of the two-story building includes jail cells with a view of the Boiling Fork Creek, and the sheriff's house, which was attached to the jail but separated by a twenty-inch-thick wall. "We also have what you might call a brag room," McNutt says proudly. "Four Tennessee governors were from Franklin County. David Crockett was from around here, too. And Andrew Jackson was a traveling judge here about that time."

Just west of Winchester on US 64 lie the remains of the Hundred Oaks Castle, one of America's last remaining castles. The thirty-room structure was built in 1891 but was devastated by fire in 1990. Listed on the National Register of Historic Places, the red brick building used to be a splendor of towers and cloisters. What's left now are the battlement tower, great hall, library, and two-story study. The building is currently not available for tours, but visitors can see the exterior and former grandeur. No plans are currently being made for the castle's renovation, but that could change in the future.

For an interesting detour, follow US 64 west to the unincorporated community of Old Salem. Beautiful farms line US 64, otherwise known as the David Crockett Highway. Sure, blossoming tobacco and corn are pretty, but what makes these farms so lovely is that they're filled with rows and rows of wildflowers.

Look for signs for Falls Mill, a beautiful working example of a water-powered grain mill built in 1873. On the National Register of Historic Places, the mill was originally a wool factory. The three-story red brick building has also housed a cotton gin and a woodworking shop. When the mill first opened, twenty-five women were paid two dollars each for a seventy-five-hour workweek making wool. The mill was restored in 1970 and named for the dancing falls of Factory Creek that rush over the old mill dam behind the building.

Owners John and Janie Lovett have reopened the site as a flour and gristmill. With the help of a full-time miller, they still mill grain on stones by waterpower from one of the largest waterwheels still operating in the country. The Lovetts, who bought the mill in 1984, have a gift and craft shop upstairs and a room housing nineteenth-century textile machinery, including an 1885 printing press, broom-making equipment, and an 1850 hand loom. The mill is open year-round for tours and hiking. Ducks and peacocks roam the grounds from which there is a remarkable view of the thirty-two-foot waterwheel and the falls.

Back in Winchester, take US 64 east through Cowan and into Sewanee. The Sewanee Natural Bridge State Natural

Falls Mill still produces old-fashioned stone-ground cornmeal

Area, just off of State 56, offers hiking trails and the enormous Sewanee Natural Bridge. A gravel and dirt pathway leads to the top of the weathered sandstone bridge and visitors can walk across the flat, narrow top and look at the ground—a *harrowing* twenty-seven feet below.

Sewanee is home to the University of the South. The campus is situated on 10,000 acres atop Tennessee's Cumberland Plateau. Founded by leaders of the Episcopal Church in 1857, the campus is an architectural replica of Oxford University in England. The university was the brainchild of Bishop Leonidas Polk of Louisiana, who in 1856 sent letters to other bishops about the church building a center of learning in the South. But Polk was killed in the Civil War, and the cornerstone, laid in 1860, was demolished by Northern troops. Charles Todd Quintard, the second Episcopal bishop of Tennessee, saved the school by preaching all over England. The bishop collected 2,500 pounds of sterling from English nobles, and between 1875 and 1915 nine major buildings were erected.

The main quadrangle of the campus is anchored by the All Saints Chapel, with its Shapard Tower in the front and Convocation Hall and Breslin Tower in the back. Both buildings are examples of Gothic architecture at its finest. Constructed in 1885, Convocation Hall and the Breslin Tower are made of locally quarried sandstone, as are many of the buildings on campus. All Saints Chapel, a full-blown cathedral, was begun in 1905 and completed in 1959. The vaulted ceilings of the nave were designed in the vein of medieval cathedrals, such as Chartres and Amiens in France. The Farish Rose Window is based on the rose window of Notre Dame de Paris in France. Twenty feet in diameter, the stained glass window is awe inspiring whether seen from the front sidewalk or from inside the nave of the chapel. Shapard Tower's design is based upon that of Saint Mary the Virgin at the University Church at Oxford University. Rising 143 feet into the sky, the tower houses the fifty-six-bell Leonidas Polk

Memorial Carillon, said to be one of the "most significant" carillons in the world.

The school's history is played out in a series of stained glass windows that line the vestibule of the chapel. They include everything from the planning of the university to the founding of the *Sewanee Review* to the time that President William Howard Taft visited the campus. Flags representing the twelve states in which owning dioceses of the university are located hang prominently in the chapel. And glass cases along the walls display articles such as a battle flag from Shiloh that was carried by the Florida regiment and an American flag that was given to the school when it was founded in 1857.

Rebel's Rest, located down the street from All Saints Chapel, is the oldest house still standing in Sewanee. Built in 1886 by Maj. George R. Fairbanks, one of the founders of the university, the fairly large log cabin was used by the Fairbankses until 1963, when the university took it over. Noted by a Tennessee marker, the house stands on the former property of Bishop Leonidas Polk. Guided tours of the campus are available by calling 615-598-1286. There is also a twenty-three-mile public hiking trail that makes a complete circle around the campus. Maps of the trail can be found at the Bishop's Common building on Georgia Avenue.

Between Sewanee and Monteagle on US 64 is a restaurant called 4 Seasons. Built by Dan Barry in 1982, the home-style-cooking restaurant looks more like a big barn. Square wooden tables, a hardwood floor perfect for dancing, and a buffet of everything from chicken and dressing to fresh fried catfish and creamed corn make for a casual, kick-off-your-shoes atmosphere.

Monteagle is home to one of only thirteen chautauquas in the country and the only one in the South. The Monteagle Sunday School Assembly is a collection of 167 Victorian, Queen Anne, and Carpenter Gothic houses built in 1882 and patterned after the New York chautauqua. Eight Christian men from Tennessee, Alabama, Kentucky, and Georgia chose Monteagle for the chautauqua, an event that combines religion with art, recreation, and education. Still active today, the chautauqua is held seven days a week from mid-June to mid-August each year. To participate, people must reside on the grounds for the duration of the educational event.

Most of the homes in this quiet community of narrow lanes and long footbridges are privately owned, except for the Adams Edgeworth Inn, built in 1896. The quaint bed and breakfast serves as the centerpiece of the area and offers rooms with fine antiques, art, sculpture, and American quilts. Open year-round, the inn offers a golf cart for visitors to use to tour the Victorian village, which is on the National Register of Historic Places.

The South Cumberland State Park Visitor Center is located between Monteagle and Tracy City on State 56. Not just a brochure pickup point, this great little museum offers geological and historical information about the 12,000-acre state park, which includes seven different areas: Grundy Lakes State Park, Grundy Forest Natural Area, Foster Falls TVA Small Wild Area, Sewanee Natural Bridge State Natural Area, Carter State Natural Area, Hawkins Cove Natural Area, and the Savage Gulf State Natural Area. Savage Gulf is named for Samuel Savage, supposedly the first settler in the gulf. The museum includes his history and a small log cabin, part of which was built in the 1800s, to show what life might have been like in "them thar hills."

The Fiery Gizzard Trail was recently listed as one of the top hiking spots in the country in a national poll by *Backpacker* magazine. The thirteen-mile trail begins at the Grundy Forest Natural Area, just outside of Tracy City, and runs south to Foster Falls. There are several theories as to how the trail got its name; the most popular concerns frontiersman Davy

Crockett. Eating dinner over a campfire with Indians, Crockett supposedly bit into a roasted wild turkey and spit out a "fiery gizzard."

Tracy City, at the intersection of State 56 and US 41, is located high on the Cumberland Plateau. It holds the distinction of having the oldest family-owned bakery in Tennessee. The Dutch Maid Bakery was established in 1902 by John Baggenstoss, a Swiss immigrant who came to America in the 1880s and settled in the nearby Swiss colony of Gruetli-Laager. A few years later, he met and married the former Louise Angst, who had immigrated to the Gruetli colony with her parents when she was seven. As a matter of fact, the two had grown up near each other in their native land, but they'd never met until they both moved to Tennessee.

A chef at the Beersheba Springs Hotel, Baggenstoss saved up $100 to start the bakery. The couple and their six sons rented a building in Tracy City, and lived upstairs and worked downstairs. The baking Baggenstosses' breads, cookies, pies, and pastries were soon the talk of the town. Albert Baggenstoss, the youngest of the six brothers, ran the bakery until his death at the age of seventy-eight in 1991. Lynn and his wife, Nelda Craig, are now up to their elbows in flour, offering the salt-rising bread, sugarplum cakes, and fruitcakes that patrons have come to love.

One of Lynn's favorite stories about the bakery is the origin of its name. "John had wanted to name it the Swiss Maid Bakery, but that name was already taken. So he said, 'OK, how about the Deutsch Maid Bakery?' But when the newspapers printed the name, they changed it to the Dutch Maid Bakery and it just stuck."

Lynn offers tours of the bakery, which includes forty-two-pound metal mixing bowls, a 1929 mixer, bread pans that date back to the 1940s, and a 1923 Traveling Tray Oven. Lighting the massive, antique oven is an event in itself. Lynn sets fire to a long stick and then places it deep inside the oven to light the burners. They turn hot and golden, row by row, as the worn metal shelves rotate slowly clockwise.

Most of the equipment is so old, Lynn says, that if anything breaks, parts have to be made. A lot of the kitchen appliances are the same ones the family used to make 12,000 loaves of bread a day for the military training base in nearby Tullahoma during World War II. Still causing anxiety for the post office, the bakery sends thousands of fruitcakes around the world during the Christmas season.

From Tracy City, take State 56 north to Altamont, the county seat of Grundy County and home to two wonderful bed and breakfasts. The Manor House, owned and operated by Harriette and Joe Gray, was built in 1885 by H. B. Northcutt. The Federal-style structure is listed on the National Register of Historic Places and features private rooms, a hearty Tennessee breakfast, and an antique shop in the house.

We stayed at The Woodlee House with Earlene Speer, a Texas-born attorney who turned the pre–Civil War home into a bed and breakfast four years ago. Built in three phases, the first part of the home, a one-room log cabin, was built before the Civil War. The exterior wall of the old log cabin is now the interior wall of the living room. The second phase, which included most of the Colonial two-story house, was added in 1895. The last additions, a living room and kitchen, were made in 1910.

One interesting aspect of the bed and breakfast is that Woodlee stipulated in his will that the house be owned only by attorneys. Speer is the third owner; her law office is downstairs. Woodlee's original law office sign hangs above the door to her secretary's office. New and old law books line the shelves. Some of the books contain Supreme Court decisions from as early as 1838. The Grundy County Courthouse was conveniently located just across the street until it was destroyed by fire in 1990.

The house offers two private bedrooms with a shared bath, antiques, a wealth of reading material, and a hearty breakfast. There's no movie theater or other entertainment for miles, so you better like who you bring. Just outside of Altamont, Swiss for "top of the mountain," is The Cumberland Craftsman. Owned by artist Ron Van Dyke, the barn-shed-shop stands along State 56, on the grounds of the former Greeter's Mill, which was in operation from 1901 to 1968. Van Dyke has set the old red Greeter steam engine back up in front. He can tell you the history of the place, back when the Greeters operated a gristmill and sawmill in Altamont. But Van Dyke's real interest is folk art. A native of Chattanooga, he moved here shortly after high school to work on his wood carvings. "I always wanted to live in the mountains," he says. "I moved here to get away from everything."

Today, the place is scattered with wood carvings, folk art, and interesting souvenirs. "I go to the salvage yards to get scrap metal and stuff," Van Dyke says. "It's hard to keep enough junk. But it's fun to see what you can find. It's like a treasure hunt. I have people who bring me stuff and I'm always finding farmers who'll sell me their piles of junk."

Some of Van Dyke's specialties include metal flowers made from tire tools and alternator sprockets with trowels for leaves, pine-knot sculptures, and intricately carved walking sticks.

Beersheba Springs, a National Historic District, lies just a few miles north on State 56. Here you'll find pre–Civil War cabins, a pre–Civil War hotel, and some stunning Tennessee countryside. The town is named for Beersheba Porter Cain of McMinnville, who found a spring in the mountain while on a business trip here with her husband. Thinking that the water was therapeutic, she returned again and again and pretty soon plenty of people were visiting the area. Cabins were built, a turnpike was forged through Cumberland Mountain by way of Beersheba Springs, and in 1839 Beersheba Springs was incorporated by the Tennessee General Assembly.

John Armfield, a young entrepreneur, moved to Beersheba Springs in 1854, bought the Beersheba Hotel, and built twenty private residences for his wealthy friends, one of whom was the Bishop Leonidas Polk, a key founder of the University of the South. In fact, the first meeting of the school's board of trustees was held at the Beersheba Hotel.

Now called the Methodist Assembly, the Beersheba Hotel still serves guests from all over. The two-story white hotel, lined with graceful porches, is open year-round. John Armfield and his faithful slave Nathan are buried in a nearby private cemetery that's surrounded by a wrought-iron gate and shaded by weeping willow trees. The hotel and cemetery are on Armfield Avenue; the pre–Civil War cabins line Dahlgreen Avenue, which runs perpendicular to Armfield. The Beersheba Springs Crafts Fair is held the fourth weekend of August each year on the grounds of the Methodist Assembly. About 14,000 people come to see the crafts and sit on the porch of the hotel and swap stories.

Near Beersheba Springs is the Savage Gulf State Natural Area, with more than 11,500 acres of bluffs and trails and plenty of waterfalls. One of the easiest and most rewarding trails in the state starts at the Stone Door Ranger Station. A one-mile hike with almost no change in elevation takes visitors to Stone Door, a startling hundred-foot-deep crevice at the crest of the Cumberland Plateau. The narrow, rocky stairway path through the mountain leads to the Savage Gulf trails. Near Stone Door are overlooks that are scenic to say the least. You can see thousands of treetops in the valley below— *way* below. In the fall, the entire area is awash with color. In the summer, don't wear perfume—bees enjoy this area as well.

Back in Altamont, take State 56 south to State 108, which takes you to Gruetli-Laager. From there, take State 111 north to Cagle and then State 8 east to US 127, which goes south to Dunlap. These small, winding roads offer delightful scenery as you wind your way down the mountainous Cumberland Plateau.

Dunlap is an annual participant in one of the country's largest continuous garage sales. The town of 3,800 people actually has traffic jams during the three-day sale, held in August, which runs along US 127 from Chattanooga all the way up to Cincinnati, Ohio.

"It started out as just an idea to motivate people to come to small towns," says Carson Camp, former mayor of Dunlap. "It's been one of the best things I've ever seen and it doesn't require a big budget. People from up north time their return trips to Florida so they can drive back on US 127 for the garage sales. I even know a man who moved here after coming to the sale."

The big event brings visitors into the town's main restaurant, Hardee's, and to the Coke Ovens National Historic Site. Dunlap, the county seat of Sequatchie County, used to be a "hot" industrial center. From 1902 to 1927, more than 250 beehive ovens were used to turn coal into coke for the iron and steel foundries in nearby Chattanooga. Built in long double rows, the ovens were each twelve-foot circles holding six tons of coal and making three tons of coke apiece. Railroad tracks ran along the top of the ovens so that railcars could dump the coal inside for a seventy-two-hour cooking period. The coke was then removed and loaded up for Chattanooga.

To get to the historic site, take US 127 to Cherry Road. Turn right onto Third, then left onto Hickory, then right onto Mountain View. Look for signs.

Today, the sixty-two-acre site, built at the turn of the century, looks like ancient ruins. Walking through the park, you can see hundreds of round sandstone and brick openings to the ovens. It is said that this area used to have a reddish glow at night. A museum, built to the scale of the former company store that served the region's miners, opened recently and houses photographs of the area.

Ironically enough, this area served as the county garbage dump for years, says Camp, who is also president of the Sequatchie Valley Historical Association. "Our members cleaned up the area, we got the photographical history of the place, and then got it on the National Register of Historic Places."

Camp, a native of Dunlap, grew up listening to his ancestors tell stories about the ovens and the coal mines. His maternal grandfather died when he was twenty-eight of "black lung" after working in the coal mines since he was a child.

One of the main sources of entertainment in the area were "incline horse" competitions, Camp says. At the end of the day, a miner would ride the rail on a small seat made of wood with a metal rower on the back and a metal shoe on the front made to fit the rail. Balancing himself with two wooden sticks, the miner would race a horse down the tracks at speeds of up to sixty miles an hour. "It was dangerous because you could tip easily and hit the crossties," says Camp. "But it was just a quick way to get home to supper. And it became a sport on the weekends."

Take US 127 south over the sparkling waters of the Sequatchie River and along Walden Ridge to Signal Mountain. From here, take US 27 south into Chattanooga, county seat of Hamilton County and the fourth largest city in the state.

Chattanooga is a city with an interesting past. Hunter Elisha Walden came through here in 1760 and left his name on Walden Ridge, which overlooks from the north the Grand Canyon of the Tennessee River. John McDonald, a Scot, established the first white settlement in 1761 when he set up a trading post, referred to as the "Old French Store."

John Ross, however, is credited with laying the foundation of the city in 1815 after setting up a trading post, called Ross's Landing, and establishing a ferry across the river. Only one-eighth Native American, Ross was Principal Chief of the Cherokee nation for forty years. The well-educated Ross served the Cherokees from the time he was nineteen until his death in 1866. The history and accomplishments of Ross are documented in the Red Clay Museum (see Chapter 5), site of the beginning of the Trail of Tears.

Chattanooga's name is supposedly an Indian expression for "rock rising to a point," referring to Lookout Mountain. The name became official on November 14, 1838. Today, you can still see where Ross first brought Chattanooga to life at Ross's Landing Park and Plaza, a $10 million project on Second Street. A unique combination of architecture, art, and history, the plaza houses one of the city's visitors centers, some gift shops, and the Tennessee Aquarium, at One Broad Street.

The lines are long and the place is packed, but the aquarium is one of the must-sees in Tennessee. Feel the mist of Cove Forest, where more than a hundred wildflowers are planted. See the underbelly and eyes of a stingray as it ascends gracefully to the surface of the water. Watch a school of brook trout swim constantly facing the current of a simulated mountain stream like a person trying to travel up a descending escalator. The aquarium offers an in-depth look at 7,000 animals—all in natural settings. The Bonnet-head sharks are in water similar to their native Gulf of Mexico; the waters of Nickajack Lake have been re-created for the carp; and the piranhas swim in waters similar to the Amazon.

The tour takes about two hours and is a visual feast of fish in every color. There are alligators, snakes, and turtles as well as other animals. And the *enormous* gray catfish will make you think twice the next time you feel something nibbling on your leg in a Tennessee lake.

One of the best views of Chattanooga is afforded by a ride on the Lookout Mountain Incline Railway, at 827 East Brow Road. Part of Chattanooga's public transportation system, the incline takes passengers a mile into the sky above the city. Its ceiling and walls lined with glass, the incline tram offers an unobstructed view of the terrain and the track, which gently slopes behind you for the first part of the ride. Somewhere past the middle of the trip, however, the tram begins to climb at a 72.7-degree angle and the track appears to drop out from under you.

If you think this sounds frightening, imagine being the first people to ride up the mountain when the incline was used here in the late nineteenth century. Passengers ascended in open-air wooden cars with nothing between them and oblivion but a handrail. The tram idea started in 1886 when some businessmen built an elaborate four-story hotel below the famous point of Lookout Mountain and then built a narrow-gauge incline railway to reach it. Meanwhile, another group of investors built yet another hotel and the Broad Gauge Railroad, which wound around the side of Lookout Mountain, covering fifteen miles and taking more than an hour to reach the top. In 1895, a new group of investors built the Lookout Mountain Incline Railway, a straight shot up the steepest part of the mountain, to connect the thriving community above to the village of St. Elmo 2,000 feet below.

The incline carries some 3,500 to 5,000 visitors up the mountainside every day. It's electric now; it used to be powered by coal furnaces at the top. The incline still uses the original double-cable system, linking cars at the top and the bottom stations and letting the "down car" pull the "up car" through the steep grades. The view from the top is still breathtaking—the Moccasin Bend of the Tennessee River, three bridges stretching across the water, and the distant mountain ranges along the Tennessee–North Carolina border.

Lookout Mountain played a crucial role in the Civil War. The Confederate and Union troops were fighting to gain control of Chattanooga, a key rail center that opened the door to the heart of the Confederacy. That meant controlling Lookout Mountain and Missionary Ridge as well. A series of battles occurred in the areas surrounding Chattanooga during the fall of 1863, one of which was the Battle of Chickamauga. One of the bloodiest battles of the Civil War, Chickamauga had more than 34,000 casualties. Surveying the carnage, Confederate Gen. William Bates called Chickamauga a "river of death."

Chickamauga National Military Park, the nation's first and oldest national military park, honors the Battle of Chickamauga and the battles for Chattanooga. Established in 1890, the huge park contains 1,400 monuments and historical markers for the Civil War battles. Located both in Chattanooga and in Georgia, the park features an eleven-mile self-guided auto tour and hiking and horseback riding trails. The park headquarters, in Georgia, features exhibits and a multimedia presentation, *Battle of Chickamauga*.

Near the bottom of the incline is St. Elmo, one of Chattanooga's first neighborhoods and the first one to get running water. On the National Register of Historic Places, the district includes restored Queen Anne, Victorian, and Tudor homes from the 1880s and crafts and collectors' shops. Established in 1879 when Col. A. M. Johnson began subdividing and developing his wife's farm, the area was originally home to Daniel Ross, John Ross's father.

One of Chattanooga's most unique offerings lies at the foot of the western slope of Lookout Mountain, at 400 Garden Road. Reflection Riding, designed like an English landscape, is a three-hundred-acre nature reserve with twelve hiking and horseback riding trails, a three-mile driving trail, grazing horses, quacking ducks, and friendly geese. Chock-full of deciduous trees and wildflowers, the park is an oasis in a town of tourism. It's beautiful and peaceful, and you don't have to be a botanical genius to appreciate the wealth of shrubs, trees, and flowers that carpet the reserve—they're all clearly marked. You'll find blue-eyed Marys and Virginia bluebells in the spring and native azaleas, mountain laurel, and yellow tulips in the summer. Civil War battle sites and Native American historical sites in the park are also clearly marked.

Chattanooga's arts district lies in the north part of the city next to the river, within sight of the city's three bridges. Built 102 years ago, the Walnut Street Bridge was recently restored and reopened as the "longest pedestrian walkway bridge in the world." On one end of the bridge, you'll find shopping and restaurants. On the other, you'll find the Hunter Museum of Art (at 10 Bluff View), a nationally acclaimed museum featuring nineteenth- and twentieth-century American art. You'll also find the Houston Antique Museum (201 High Street), the River Gallery (400 East Second Street), and a public sculpture garden.

The Houston Antique Museum is nationally known among collectors and dealers in glassware. Anna Safley Houston collected antiques all her life, but her particular passion was pitchers. When she died in 1951, she donated her collection, which includes 15,000 antique pitchers, to her adopted home of Chattanooga. Several thousand of them are on display, in the cupboards, on the shelves, and hanging from the ceiling.

A short walk up the street is the Hunter Museum of Art. Housed in an opulent Classic Revival mansion built between 1904 and 1906 by Coca-Cola magnate George Thomas Hunter, the museum sits on a former Cherokee holy place. During the Civil War, the mansion served as a battery for both the Union and Confederate armies.

Today, the Hunter features paintings by Mary Cassatt, Andrew Wyeth, and Winslow Homer; a portrait by John Singer Sargent; black-and-white photographs by Alfred Stieglitz; Native American artifacts; bronze sculptures; and oil paintings by Frederic Remington. Located on a bluff above the river, the mansion is furnished with priceless antiques throughout and huge, ornate mirrors in the foyer. The house alone would be worth seeing; the art is just icing on the cake.

Almost across the street from the museum, at 412 East Second Street, is the Bluff View & Tea Room, one of the most wonderful places in Tennessee to spend the night. The red brick, white-columned Colonial Revival mansion offers a spectacular view of the river, a gourmet breakfast, and three bedrooms, all decorated with fine antiques and an eye for detail. A public sculpture garden lies next to Bluff View and overlooks the river.

Just a few blocks away, at 414 Vine Street, is the Vine Street Market, a restaurant and shop offering an array of jams, specialty coffees, and sauces. Formerly a grocery store, the building now has a small, barn-wood-paneled, comfortable dining room with swinging saloon doors at the entrance. During the day, the restaurant offers soups, salads, and sandwiches. Each night, the chef prepares a poultry, a fish, and a red meat offering. Our dinner of fresh salad with homemade dressing, tender salmon, and spicy chicken was excellent. One of the restaurant's most popular dishes is the halibut with crabmeat, capers, and a lemon beurre blanc served with asparagus.

One of the nation's oldest manufacturing cities, Chattanooga has its share of warehouses and mills, but the downtown area has some architectural gems, many of which are on the National Register of Historic Places. The beautifully restored Radisson Read House, on the corner of Broad Street and M. L. King Boulevard, was built in 1847 by Thomas Crutchfield. As the Crutchfield House it served as the political, social, and economic heart of Chattanooga at the time. In 1872, Dr. and Mrs. John T. Read renamed the hotel The Read House. When the ornate Georgian-style structure was opened again in 1926, the *New York Times* described it as a "monument to good taste."

On Broad Street there's the Tivoli Theatre, which has been called the "Jewel of the South." A magnificent old theater still in use today, the Tivoli was built in 1921 and has been restored several times over the years. When the theater first opened, people came here to watch motion pictures. The theater still shows movie classics, but it is also used for Chattanooga Symphony and Opera performances, school programs, and business functions.

If shopping's your bag, you'll love what they've done with the once empty turn-of-the-century railroad warehouses in the heart of downtown. A little paint here, a little marble there, and more than thirty designer outlet stores make Warehouse Row some of the best and most aesthetically pleasing shopping in the South.

Of course, you can't leave without seeing the Chattanooga Choo-Choo, at 1400 Market Street. Built in 1909, the original terminal station was the hub of commerce, welcoming thousands of travelers during the age of railroad. The totally restored train station now serves as a beautiful Holiday Inn, offering more than 300 guest rooms and forty-five sleeping parlors aboard authentic railcars. The Choo-Choo also houses one of the largest model railroad exhibits in the world that is open to the public. A joint venture between the Chattanooga Area Model Railroad Club and the Chattanooga Choo-Choo Company, the display took more than 33,000 man-hours to create and is estimated to have cost $500,000.

The first part of the exhibit is a true-to-life layout of Chattanooga, from the Missionary Ridge train tunnel, which was used by all south- and east-bound traffic in 1849; to Lookout Mountain; to the busy downtown. The second part is a made-up portion of the Cumberland Mountains, poking fun at shotgun weddings, town drunks, and moonshine making. Encased by glass, the exhibit includes more than 3,000 feet of track, 150 switches, 120 locomotives of all types, and 1,000 freight cars. You don't have to wait long at any point of the exhibit to see or hear a train coming around the bend.

Other people-packed offerings in Chattanooga include Ruby Falls (on the Lookout Mountain Scenic Highway), a 145-foot multicolored flowing waterfall that draws some 400,000 visitors annually; the Confederama (3742 Tennessee Avenue), a three-dimensional presentation of Chattanooga's history featuring 5,000 miniature figures and details of major battles in 1863; and the Tennesseee Valley Railroad (4119 Cromwell Road), which offers excursions on the largest operating historic railroad in the South. We didn't have time for those sites, but they might interest you.

Chattanooga is a popular place to be in the fall, when the mountains become lakes of red, orange, and gold leaves. One of the city's biggest events, the Fall Color Cruise and Folk Festival, is held the last two weekends in October and includes crafts, music, food, and cruises aboard the Southern Belle Riverboat on the Tennessee River and Nickajack Lake.

In the Area

Adams Edgeworth Inn (Monteagle): 615-924-2669

Bluff View & Tea Room (Chattanooga): 615-265-5033

Chattanooga Choo-Choo (Chattanooga):
   615-266-5500

Chickamauga National Military Park (Chattanooga):
   615-752-5213

Confederama (Chattanooga): 615-821-2812

The Cumberland Craftsman (Altamont): 615-692-3595

Dutch Maid Bakery (Tracy City): 615-592-3171

Falls Mill (Belvidere): 615-469-7161 + museum

4 Seasons (Monteagle): 615-598-5544

Houston Antique Museum (Chattanooga): 615-267-7176

Hundred Oaks Castle (Winchester): 615-967-0100

Hunter Museum of Art (Chattanooga): 615-267-0968

The Iron Kettle (Lynchburg): 615-759-4274

Jack Daniel Distillery (Lynchburg): 615-759-4221

Lookout Mountain Incline Railway (Chattanooga):
    615-821-4224

Lynchburg Ladies' Handiwork (Lynchburg): 615-759-7919

The Manor House (Altamont): 615-692-3153

Miss Mary Bobo's (Lynchburg): 615-759-7394

Old Jail Museum (Winchester): 615-967-0524

Radisson Read House (Chattanooga): 615-266-4121

Reflection Riding (Chattanooga): 615-821-1160

River Gallery (Chattanooga): 615-267-7353

Ruby Falls, Lookout Mountain Scenic Highway
    (Chattanooga): 615-821-2544

South Cumberland State Park Visitor Center (Monteagle):
    615-924-2980

Tennessee Aquarium (Chattanooga): 800-262-0695

Tennessee Valley Railroad (Chattanooga): 615-849-8028

Tivoli Theatre (Chattanooga): 615-757-5050

University of the South (Sewanee): 615- 598-1286

Vine Street Market (Chattanooga): 615-267-8165

Warehouse Row Factory Outlets (Chattanooga):
    615-267-1111

The Woodlee House (Altamont): 615-692-2368

2 ~

Greeneville

to

Elizabethton

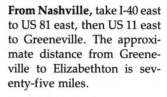

From Nashville, take I-40 east to US 81 east, then US 11 east to Greeneville. The approximate distance from Greeneville to Elizabethton is seventy-five miles.

Highlights: *The Andrew Johnson National Historic Site in Greeneville; Sycamore Shoals State Historic Area, site of the formation of the Watauga Association and the Doe River Covered Bridge in Elizabethton; and the historic homes and National Storytelling Festival of Jonesborough, Tennessee's oldest town.*

Traveling in East Tennessee is like opening a book of the state's history to the first chapter. White settlers came to the area in the 1700s, risking their lives, families, and fortunes to cross the Appalachian Mountains and settle in the "unknown west" of East Tennessee.

This area saw the creation in 1772 of the Watauga Association, America's first free and independent government. In 1784, three East Tennessee counties, then a part of North Carolina, attempted to create the State of Franklin. Historic leaders such as John Sevier, Andrew Johnson, William Blount, and Davy Crockett took the strong people of the early frontier through Indian attacks, hostile political climates, and changing times.

Greeneville, the second oldest town in Tennessee, played a major role in the state's history. Founded in 1781, the town was originally part of North Carolina. Greeneville became part of Tennessee when the state was admitted to the Union in 1796. The town served as stomping grounds for a famous tailor. At the age of fifteen, Andrew Johnson ran away from his hometown of Raleigh, North Carolina, and a master tailor to whom he had been apprenticed. Our nation's seventeenth president set up his own tailor shop in a log cabin in Greeneville in 1831.

Johnson never received any formal education, but with the help of his wife, Eliza McCardle Johnson, he learned to read. He would also pay people fifty cents a day to read to him while he worked. From 1831 to 1843, Johnson sewed and talked politics with the men of the town in his shop, which became a center of activity.

Twenty-two years later, after a stint as Greeneville's mayor and Tennessee's only military governor, Johnson would become president of the United States, after Abraham Lincoln's assassination. And he would also become the only president ever to be impeached.

A visit to the Andrew Johnson National Historic Site, located on College and Depot streets, is enlightening. Often viewed as the president who destroyed the South with Reconstruction policies, Johnson is shown here in a different light. The museum tells the story of a champion of the working class—a man with compassion and integrity who believed strongly in the Constitution and its execution, no matter the personal price. Included in the historic site are the homestead, museum, his tailor shop, and Johnson's early residence. An impressive red brick home on South Main Street, Johnson's homestead was where he lived with his family until his death in 1875. The house features unusually short door frames to fit the people of the time. The Johnsons' grave in Andrew Johnson National Cemetery is adorned with a stately Italian marble grave marker with the inscription, "His faith in the people never wavered."

Just across the way from the Andrew Johnson National Historic Site, at 212 East Depot Street, is Ye Olde Tourist Trappe. The shop is adorable if you like country crafts. They have shelves and shelves of everything from wooden statues to clothes to bread warmers—all handmade.

If you feel like walking, almost all of Greeneville's history happened within a few blocks of the Andrew Johnson National Historic Site. "A Walk With the President," an organized two-hour walking tour of historic Greeneville, is offered Monday through Saturday, originating at the Greene County Chamber of Commerce at 207 North Main Street. An advantage to the organized tour is seeing the interiors of some buildings, such as the Old County Jail and the Capital of the Lost State of Franklin, which aren't otherwise open to the public.

Start on Main Street, a beautiful, rolling street lined with historic buildings. A historical marker stands in front of the Greeneville/Greene County Library, on North Main Street. The building sits almost on top of The Big Spring, a juncture of two Indian trails that served as a stopping place for tired travelers. When some Scotch-Irish pioneers found the spring and decided to settle, Greeneville was established. This spring was the city's major source of water for more than 150 years. Today, the pretty little stream runs behind the library and under a romantic footbridge. Carry some old bread in your pocket—this is a great hangout for ducks.

From here, travel one block west to the Capital of the Lost State of Franklin, on College Street, across from the Town Hall. A small reproduction log cabin sits off the road and under some trees. A historical marker tells the fascinating story of a group of people who longed for the creation of a new state, separate from North Carolina.

Next stop on this unofficial tour is the Old Greene County Stone Jail, which lies just behind the courthouse, off Depot Street. Originally built in 1804–1805, the structure was similar to old Roman jails. The single-story building, which was constructed of limestone rock, was placed almost on Richland Creek so that water could be channeled to enter and flow through a trough in the stone floor to carry away human waste. In 1838, the original building was torn down and moved, stone by stone, to its present site. A red brick second story was added in 1882. The century-old jail is essentially the same, except for some new plumbing and electrical wiring. We peeked in the windows, but all we could see was pigeons . . . jailbirds.

From the jail, take Depot Street east and then head north on Main Street to the Greeneville Cumberland Presbyterian Church at 201 North Main Street. The Civil War left its mark on this church, built in 1841, in the form of a cannonball lodged in the upper right side of the front door. The Greek Revival church, still in use today, served as both a hospital and a stable during the Civil War.

St. James Episcopal Church, across the way on North Main Street, was built in 1850. Go inside the white frame structure and look at the beautiful walnut woodwork and pews and the slave gallery. The church has the oldest pipe organ in the state.

From Greeneville, travel just a few miles east on US 11 to Tusculum, home of America's oldest Presbyterian college. Founded in 1794, Tusculum College continues to draw students from across the country. In 1980, eight red brick buildings and the stone archway that marks the front entrance to the college were established as the Tusculum College Historic District by the National Trust for Historic Preservation. The lovely campus is secluded and covered with trees. It includes the Samuel Doak House, built in 1818 for the first president of the college. He was an early Presbyterian minister who regularly preached to travelers at the Big Spring in Greeneville. Today, the building houses the Doak-Johnson Heritage Museum, which features exhibits showing the development of culture and education in the area.

From Tusculum, take US 11 east toward Jonesborough. Then take Old State Route 34 to the Davy Crockett Road, then turn right to go to the Davy Crockett Birthplace State Park. Contrary to legend and hype, Davy Crockett was not born on a mountaintop. The warrior, hero, and backwoods statesman was born on August 17, 1786, along the banks of Nolichucky River, near the mouth of Limestone Creek.

The state park pays homage to Crockett, a man respected for his sincerity and bravery, with a reproduction log cabin, similar to the one he was born in along these waters. The simple cabin contains a wooden table with dishes and some furniture. Visitors can look inside the cabin through a metal fence at the entrance. The sixty-five-acre park has a swimming pool, as well as a large campground, hiking trails, picnic areas near the river, and a museum/visitors center. Here you'll find on display the kinds of things that Crockett would have actually used—a flop hat, a broadax, a liquor jug, a type of top hat, a tobacco twist, and a coonskin hat. A television monitor plays footage of film stars, such as the legendary John Wayne, depicting the legendary Crockett. The crafty hunter and Indian fighter died at the age of forty-nine at the Alamo, helping Texas win independence from Mexico in 1836.

From the park, take Davy Crockett Road to Old State Route 34 toward Washington College. The two-lane road winds past Victorian homes, big plantations, and summer flowers waving in the wind. After you pass Washington College Church, turn right onto Washington College Road, which will take you past the old-fashioned red brick buildings of

Washington College Academy. Originally established in 1780, the college has graduated 22 college presidents, 28 members of Congress, 3 governors, 63 physicians, 16 missionaries, 162 ministers, and many judges, lawyers, editors, and teachers. "I think one of the reasons many people came here is that for many years it was the only school for classical learning west of the Allegheny Mountains," says John Cheska, president of Washington College Academy. "Theodore Roosevelt said the college played a major role in the settlement of the West by providing professionals—doctors, lawyers, and ministers."

Some interesting spots on the campus include the Salem Graveyard, where Samuel and Jane Doak are buried. Doak became the preacher at Salem Presbyterian Church in 1780 and later helped found this school and Tusculum College. The church, built in place of the original Salem Presbyterian Church in the late 1800s, has an eye-catching round stained glass window and massive round brick columns. Harris Hall, which serves as a women's dormitory, was built in 1842; it was used, at different times, as barracks for both Union and Confederate soldiers during the Civil War.

Continue east on Old State Route 34 to Telford, a small community named for Colonel Telford, who established the Telford Agricultural Manufacturing Company here in about 1876. His three-story white clapboard building still stands, but it's vacant. The Telford Grocery, at 125 Mill Street, is still quite busy, however. Built in 1916, it was the first store between the towns of Greeneville and Jonesborough to have a gas pump. Housed in a two-story white building, the grocery is now run by John and Sandra Gunter. They have groceries, a small delicatessen, and just about every beer imaginable. A black-and-white TV sits near the front counter, and there's a pool table in the back.

From Telford, travel along Old State Route 34 east to Jonesborough, the oldest town in Tennessee. Carved out of the wilderness in 1779, Jonesborough is sometimes referred to as the "Mother of Tennessee." It was founded by the North Carolina Assembly and named in honor of Willie Jones, a prominent patriot and statesman.

Jonesborough has always been the Washington County seat, even though there's a Washington County courthouse in both Jonesborough and Johnson City. In 1784, the town also served as the capital of the Lost State of Franklin, mentioned earlier.

Walking in downtown Jonesborough is like traveling a hundred years back into the past. The town is practically a living museum of mid-nineteenth-century architecture, with many of its homes dating from the Civil War. The town became the first official historic district in Tennessee in 1969.

Jonesborough's courthouse, a majestic red brick building with Neoclassical lines, was built in 1913 and restored in 1987. Chester Inn, the oldest frame structure in town, was built before 1800 by Dr. William P. Chester. It has served as a tavern, an inn, an apartment house, a library, a specialty shop, and an office. Many a traveler has spent time on the long porch watching the townsfolk go by. Presidents Andrew Jackson, James K. Polk, and Andrew Johnson all stayed here at one time or another.

Three of Jonesborough's churches date back to the 1840s; two of them still display the galleries built to accommodate slaves before the Civil War. Jonesborough Female Academy, a small brick building built in about 1834, is on College Street. The Holston Baptist Female Institute, a two-story brick structure on Main Street, opened in 1854 but closed during the Civil War. It reopened after the war and was run as the Holston Male Institute until 1876, when it was sold to the

Quakers to be used as a school for recently freed slaves and their children.

The Old Yellow Vic at 411 West Main Street, is a two-story cozy Victorian bed and breakfast built in 1887 and now owned by Sonya Stacy. All of the rooms have a lived-in, cared-for feel, are decorated with antiques, and have high ceilings and wooden floors. There are no TVs or radios to distract you—just front-porch swings and a friendly town of people waiting to say "Howdy." A couple of times a day you can hear a train in the distance. And the country breakfasts of bacon, fresh fruit, and shortbread are so good you'll want to duplicate them at home.

Stacy opened her home to guests a few years ago because visitors needed a place to stay. "It's really not just a business," says Stacy, a lively woman who also deals in antique furniture restoration. "I enjoy the people who come through so much. One family stays with me every year—they've become extended family."

The Old Yellow Vic is the perfect place to be when visiting historic Jonesborough. It's within walking distance of most sites and a good (although pricey) restaurant—the Parson's Table. Located at 102 Woodrow Avenue, behind the court-house off Main Street, the restaurant was built in 1874. Back then, the only thing the Gothic-style building served was sermons—it was the first Christian church. Today, the upscale restaurant serves everything from crepes to smoked salmon to juicy steaks. They don't serve wine, but they'll be glad to chill a bottle you've brought. Be sure to make reservations far in advance, especially if you're visiting during one of the town's big events.

Speaking of which, Jonesborough Days is an annual three-day affair held around Independence Day. The event draws thousands of people to this town of 3,500 and includes an old-timer's parade, children's games, a barbecue, arts and crafts, live music, clogging, a talent contest, a street dance, a flea market, and fireworks at midnight on the Fourth of July.

Jonesborough hosts another three-day festival the first weekend of October that lures people by the droves to the small town. The National Storytelling Festival began as a small-time event in 1973. Jimmy Neil Smith, a high school journalism teacher, came up with the idea of such a festival to raise money for the town. Sixty people came the first year and gathered around a hay wagon on the courthouse lawn to hear a banker, a farmer, a professor, and a former congressman spin yarns.

From those humble beginnings, the festival, which is sponsored by the National Association for the Preservation and Perpetuation of Storytelling (NAPPS), is now considered the country's oldest and most prestigious storytelling event, attracting almost 7,000 people each year. More than eighty storytellers share folk and fairy tales from many cultures, personal narratives, historical accounts, tall tales, updated classics, Native American myths, cowboy poetry, Appalachian Jack tales, Cajun stories, ghost stories, and children's stories. Make plans early—at least a year in advance— to attend. Stacy says, "Almost every hotel from here to Knoxville will be booked. The storytelling is always wonderful and people who come to the festival fall in love with Jonesborough and want to come back."

Other offerings in the area include the Jonesborough/ Washington County History Museum, located in the Jonesborough Visitors Center at 117 Boone Street. The museum includes an introductory slide show and historical items such as a wooden washing machine, a corn husk broom, a saddle pack that would have served as a doctor's bag, antique quilts, and craft-making programs.

The Historic Jonesborough Visitors Center offers a guided walking tour, "Discover Jonesborough's Times and Tales."

Another tall tale unfolds at the National Storytelling Festival

The two-hour tour includes four historic buildings—two historic homes, one church, and the Christopher Taylor Log House. The tour, bringing the history of each building to life through storytelling, was named Tennessee's most outstanding cultural program in 1992 by the Tennessee Association of Museums.

From Jonesborough, take Old Jonesborough Highway toward Johnson City, a Washington County town established in 1870. The earliest white settlers to the area were John Finley, James Needham, Gabriel Arthur, and Daniel Boone— hunters and adventurers. William Bean was probably the first permanent settler—he built a cabin on the Watauga River at the mouth of Boone's Creek in 1769. The town was named after Henry Johnson, who came to the area in 1856. He built a home, the community's first general store, and a railroad depot at his own expense when the East Tennessee, Virginia and Georgia Railroad was built through Brush Creek. After the Civil War, other small stores and a restaurant were opened—all built around the public square.

Johnson City is home to East Tennessee State University, a school of about 11,000 students, founded in 1911. Some of the school's original buildings still standing include Gilbreath Hall, now housing the theater and computer laboratory facilities; Carter Hall, a women's residence hall; and the dining hall, now a College of Medicine. Most of the campus looks modern, especially the mammoth Memorial Center, a sprawling blue concrete and steel structure with a gold dome big enough to fit over a small town. Used for athletic events and convocation, among other things, the center can hold about 12,000 people.

Also located in Johnson City is the Tipton-Haynes Historical Farm, formerly owned by Col. John Tipton, Jr., one of the founding fathers of Tennessee, and Confederate Sen. Landon C. Haynes. Located at 2620 Roan Street, off County 107, the farm was the site of the 1788 Battle of the Lost State of Franklin, mentioned earlier, which ended with the dissolution of the state of Franklin. Today, the farm is a peaceful place with acres of green grass, an herb garden, ten original and restored buildings, a cave, a nature trail, and spinning and weaving demonstrations in the loom house.

From Johnson City, make your way north to Piney Flats on US 11E. The four-lane blacktop winds past businesses and over Boone Lake. Start looking for signs to Rocky Mount, the first capitol of the southwest territory. Built in 1770 by William Cobb, an early immigrant from eastern North Carolina, the two-story log house features nine rooms, pine paneling, and real glass windows. It was considered a mansion by frontier standards.

Cobb opened his home to many a traveler—some strangers, others friends. Andrew Jackson was a regular visitor. So were Daniel Boone, John Sevier, and Sam Houston. Probably the most famous visitor, however, was William Blount, appointed Territorial Governor and Superintendent of Indian Affairs in 1790 by President George Washington, and his family stayed with the Cobbs for eighteen months while his house was being built in Knoxville. During that time, the home served as the capitol of "The Territory of the United States south of the River Ohio."

The home looks pretty good, considering it's the oldest original territorial capitol in the United States and one of the oldest buildings still standing in the state. After Blount left, Rocky Mount continued to be a place of importance. It was a frequent stopping place for travelers pioneering the western lands of Middle Tennessee and beyond. Rocky Mount was on the stagecoach route between Philadelphia and Nashville and it served as a U.S. post office from 1838 to 1847.

A visit to Rocky Mount includes a one-hour tour of the home, with its eighteenth-century family furniture, the work shed, a separate kitchen, and several barns. The visit begins with a knock on the Cobbs' front door. It's 1791 and "the Cobbs are in." Men and women dressed in period clothing carry on much as the Cobbs would have done had you been a guest in the home more than two centuries ago. Aunt Jane, one of the neighbors, talks about the history of the furnishings and gives away family secrets, such as where cousin

Andrew Jackson kept his jug of whiskey. The cook gives a tour of the herb garden and kitchen, with its old-time cooking utensils. Another character demonstrates how linen dresses and linsey-woolsey covers were made on a loom in the workroom.

Emily McClellan, who has been playing the part of Barsheba Cobb for twenty-two years, says that if people can get into it, they really enjoy the first-person interpretation. "One day I was just so tired I didn't want to give any more tours," says McClellan, pushing her gray hair under her bonnet. "And then I saw a family walking toward the house. When the man came to the door, he said, 'Mrs. Cobb, we were traveling in a wagon and it broke down. We saw the smoke from your chimney and walked over. We're really sorry to bother you.' It just lifted my spirits."

From Piney Flats, take US 11 east to Bluff City and then US 19 east to Elizabethton. The four-lane divided highway, flanked on either side by scattered homes, rolls into town at the foot of Holston Mountain and crosses the enchanting Watauga River.

Elizabethton is the county seat of Carter County, home of the Watauga Association, the "first free and independent government in America." Formed in 1772, four years before the signing of the Declaration of Independence, the Watauga Association was the first permanent American settlement outside of the original thirteen colonies.

The history of the association, the first to use the majority-rule system of American democratic government, is preserved at the Sycamore Shoals State Historic Area, at 1651 West Elk Avenue. The park includes a museum, picnic grounds, and a re-creation of historic Fort Watauga at the head of the Shoals on the Watauga River. In March 1775, Sycamore Shoals was the site of the largest private or corporate real estate transaction in U.S. history, the Transylvania

Purchase. The Transylvania Company purchased more than 20 million acres of land—most of present-day Kentucky and Tennessee—from the Cherokee Indians for 2,000 pounds of sterling silver and 8,000 pounds of goods.

After a tour of Sycamore Shoals, stroll on over to the Doe River Covered Bridge, believed to be the oldest such bridge still in use in the state. At the corner of US 19E and Elk Street, the century-old white clapboard covered bridge stretches gracefully across 134 feet of water. Originally constructed in 1882 for a mere $3,000, the bridge is made entirely of wood, except for the steel pikes that fasten together the massive oak pieces used in the floor. The bridge is listed on the Historic Engineering Record and the National Register of Historic Sites.

We arrived at the bridge at the end of a hot July day after getting lost in a car with no air-conditioning. We parked near the grassy banks of the river, where people were picnicking and swimming. The late afternoon sun played on the water of the Doe River and the graceful bridge stretched out before us—a symbol of timelessness. We slipped off our shoes and let the cool water soothe our souls.

In the Area

Carter County Chamber of Commerce (Elizabethton):
  615-543-2122

Davy Crockett Birthplace State Park (Limestone):
  615-257-2167

Doak-Johnson Heritage Museum (Tusculum):
  615-636-7300

East Tennessee State University (Johnson City):
  615-929-4112

Elizabethton / Carter County Chamber of Commerce
  (Elizabethton): 615-543-2122

Greene County Chamber of Commerce (Greeneville):
615-638-4111

Greeneville Cumberland Presbyterian Church (Greeneville):
615-638-4119

Johnson City Convention & Visitors Bureau (Johnson City):
615-727-5800

Andrew Johnson National Historic Site (Greeneville):
615-638-3551

Jonesborough / Washington County History Museum
(Jonesborough): 615-753-9775

Historic Jonesborough Visitors Center (Jonesborough):
615-753-5961

National Association for the Preservation and Perpetuation
of Storytelling (Jonesborough): 615-753-2171

The Old Yellow Vic (Jonesborough): 615-753-2501,
615-753-9558

The Parson's Table (Jonesborough): 615-753-8002

Rocky Mount (Piney Flats): 615-538-7396

Sycamore Shoals State Historic Area (Elizabethton):
615-543-5808

Telford Grocery (Telford): 615-753-3883

Tipton-Haynes Historical Farm (Johnson City): 615-926-3631

Tusculum College (Tusculum): 615-636-7300

Ye Olde Tourist Trappe (Greeneville): 615-639-1567

3 ~

Knoxville

to

Jamestown

From Chattanooga, take I-75 north, which merges with I-40 east just west of Knoxville. Follow I-40 into Knoxville. The total trip length from Knoxville to Jamestown is ninety-six miles.

Highlights: *James White's Fort, Blount Mansion, and the Old City, all in Knoxville; the Museum of Appalachia in Norris; the American Museum of Science and Energy in Oak Ridge; the Victorian colony of Rugby and the Gray Gables Bed and Breakfast; the World Pumpkin Weigh-off in Allardt; and the Highland Manor Winery and Mark Twain Park in Jamestown.*

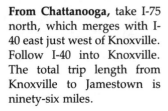

To capture the true flavor of Knoxville, visit during a University of Tennessee football game weekend. The entire town is ORANGE—safety orange hats, T-shirts, sweatshirts, flags, pom-poms, and vans—all to support the University of Tennessee Vols football team. The school's Neyland Stadium holds 96,000; dedicated fans drive from all over the country to see their team play. Walking around town the day of their season opener, my husband and I were the only ones wearing a color you couldn't hunt in.

Long before commerce and football frenzy made Knoxville Tennessee's third-largest city, the area was a lush green valley inhabited by the Cherokee Indians. Gen. James White, founder of Knoxville, and his family were the first white settlers to make a home here in the wilderness. White owned most of what would eventually become Knoxville. When he built his log home here in 1786, his closest neighbors were Cherokee Indians. Gradually, other white settlers started moving into the territory; they would often stay with the Whites, prompting White to build three log guest houses and enclose the complex with a stockade fence.

A tour of the James White Fort, at 205 East Hill Avenue, includes a beautifully manicured lawn, kitchen, the three guest log cabins, and the Whites' original main log cabin. A museum, blacksmith shop, smokehouse, and loom house were all added later to hold artifacts from the period. All the buildings are surrounded by a reproduction stockade fence. "A lot of people think he put up a stockade fence because of the Indians, but we think it was because of the bears," explained Gladys Wright, our tour guide. "They killed 200 bears the first summer alone. Besides, White had little ones and this was wilderness back then."

The kitchen includes a chest for storing pounds of flour, an open-hearth fireplace lined with drying fruits and vegetables, a cupboard covered in buttermilk paint dyed with the juice of pokeberries, and the Whites' original pineapple butter mold. The great room of the main log cabin features White's desk, the couple's original cherry wedding table, an eight-day Seth Thomas clock made before the Civil War, and family portraits. The bedroom features several period beds with feather mattresses and linsey-woolsey coverlets.

William Blount, who served as the territorial governor from 1791 to 1796, chose a beautiful spot along the Tennessee River for Blount Mansion, at 200 West Hill Avenue, a Colonial-style, two-story home. Today, the mansion, across the street from the high-rise Union Planter's Building, is as much a novelty amid fast-paced city life as it was on the open plain at the end of the eighteenth century. Cherokee Indians sup-posedly called Blount Mansion the "house of many eyes," because they had never seen so many windows in one house.

Drying herbs hang in the Blount kitchen near the open-hearth fireplace, where their head cooking slave would have prepared the meals. The Blounts reportedly had thirty slaves, many of whom would have lived above the kitchen.

The former governor's office is simply furnished, with a wooden desk, some books, and an American flag. This is where Blount (who would later serve as the first U.S. senator from Tennessee), Andrew Jackson, and others drafted the Tennessee State Constitution in 1796—the year Tennessee became a state.

The University of Tennessee at Knoxville was established as Blount College in 1794. In 1826, the campus was moved to the forty-acre tract it now occupies, which is known as "The Hill." In 1892, the board of trustees took actions to admit women, but it is believed that women were allowed to take college preparatory classes at the school as early as 1840, which would make it the first in the United States to open its doors to women.

Today, the school has a student population of 25,000. You'll find a lot of those students hanging out in the Old City District, at the intersection of Jackson Avenue and Central Street downtown. The Old City is a refurbished area of build-ings and warehouses that was the center of commerce during the industrial period. Housed in the original nineteenth-century brick buildings, Old City is a three-block area of eth-nic restaurants and trendy stores offering everything from tie-dyed T-shirts to nouveau art. At night, it's a place to share a cup of coffee at the Java Coffee House or catch some live music at Manhattan's Restaurant or hear jazz at Lucille's Restaurant or The Black Sheep Cafe. And it's always a good place to watch people.

Another great place for people watching is the Knoxville Zoo, on Prosser Road. Watch a child try to brush a goat's hair in the petting zoo. Or hear children squeal when the 420-pound gorilla lumbers over to the window and looks *right at them*. The Knoxville Zoo offers more than a thousand animal exhibits; it is nationally known for its collection of reptiles and big cats, including lions, tigers, leopards, cheetahs, and pumas. Ravi, a captivating white tiger, is the zoo's prize attraction.

Other attractions in Knoxville include: Marble Springs, 1220 West Gov. John Sevier Highway in Knoxville, the summer home of John Sevier, Tennessee's first governor; The Tennessee Theatre, a rococo-style theater built in 1928 at 604 Gay Street; the Sunsphere, a 266-foot structure built during the World's Fair, which was held here in 1982; the Frank H. McClung Museum on the University of Tennessee campus, which features displays of anthropology, archaeology, and geology as well as decorative and fine arts; the Knoxville Museum of Art (410 Tenth Street); and the Ijams Nature Center (2915 Island Home Avenue). In April, Knoxville hosts the Dogwood Arts Festival, a two-week extravaganza of music, dance, crafts, fun, and, of course, trails and trails of blooming dogwood trees.

From Knoxville, take US 441 north to Norris, a town of about a thousand people, built by the Tennessee Valley Authority in 1934. It was designed to be an example of sound community development—with a belt of parkways and farm-lands around the town to protect the city's water supply. The town's main attraction is the Museum of Appalachia (on State 61), which has been described by the *New York Times* as "the star-spangled banner from the country's pioneer past." Founded by John Rice Irwin in the 1960s, the sixty-five-acre farm includes some thirty authentic log structures, each one

Listen for the fiddles at the Museum of Appalachia

showing a different facet of the life of the mountain people. Over the years, Irwin has collected about 250,000 objects.

"I got started in this because of my interest in the people of the region," says Irwin, a native of the area. "As a child, I hunted with them, fished with them, worked for them on their farms, and did all of the things that had been done for thousands of years—like planting corn by hand and cutting wheat with a cradle. Later on, when I was superintendent of schools in Anderson County, I started buying different things from interesting families. I just kept on collecting. Most museums try to collect the very best. But I try to collect what represents the region."

The Museum of Appalachia Hall of Fame, a country home containing artifacts and memorabilia of the mountain lifestyle, is the first stop on the tour. There's a huge corncrib, a bearskin coat, home furnishings, musical instruments, and a grandfather clock said to have belonged to Sam Houston. Unlike the items displayed in other museums, those in this folk museum are accompanied by hand-written descriptions and histories—all supplied by Irwin. "I've always tried to tie the item to the person," he says. "For example, I have an ornately carved walking stick near my desk that was owned by a Civil War veteran. The bottom part of it is burned, so apparently, when he got up in age, he would sit by the fire and, instead of using a poker, he would poke at the fire with his stick. I like to know who each thing belonged to and to whom it was passed—who cared for it—because once you separate the history from the item, then to a great extent, you've destroyed the item."

Irwin includes the histories of many of the Appalachian people as well. The exhibits pay tribute to people such as Cordell Hull, the nation's secretary of state under President Franklin D. Roosevelt; bluegrass great Uncle Dave Macon; the Whittlers of Appalachia; World War I hero Sgt. Alvin C. York; and Alex Stewart, a well digger, coal miner, mountain philosopher, wood-carver, and recipient of one of the first sixteen National Fellowship Awards in 1983 from the National Endowment for the Arts.

One of the most touching displays in the Hall of Fame tells the story of Luther Clear, a man who carved wooden toys for his only grandson, Luther Pyles. The carpenter loved his grandson dearly and spent most of his time with him. When Clear went blind in 1926, his grandson was the only one who could lead him around the farm and to rest against his special birch tree. When Pyles was called away to serve in World War II, his grandfather died almost immediately of sadness.

There's also a huge display of mountain instruments made out of everything from ironing boards to cigar boxes. The walls are lined with a bedpan banjo, a cookiebox banjo, a matchstick guitar, a tobacco box mandolin, and a hammered dulcimer.

The Display Building includes exhibits on spinning and weaving, shoemaking, and carpentry, as well as a country store and a large folk art collection. Cedar Creek Charlie Fields, who moved to the area from Lebanon, Virginia, in 1970, was famous for painting everything—including his house, clothes, shoes, and *himself*—in red, white, and blue polka dots. Troy Webb, an "untaught and unpredictable" artist, is famous for his simple, blocklike wood carvings of everyday people. And Harrison Mayes was famous for promoting God on signs, wood carvings, and concrete crosses erected all over the world.

Other buildings on the tour include a smokehouse, a chapel, a schoolhouse, blacksmith shops, and privies. Old-time musicians play the banjo, guitar, and fiddle as you walk past planted gardens, roosting chickens, sheep, and colorful peacocks. It's a great place for city dwellers to see tasseling corn and the brilliant blues of a rooster's plume.

The museum is also the site of the Tennessee Fall Homecoming Celebration, held every October. Voted one of the Top Twenty October events in the Southeast by the Southeast Tourism Society for the past eight years, the event includes old-time mountain music and Appalachian crafts.

From Norris, take State 61 south to Clinton and then State 95 to Oak Ridge, the "Energy Capital of the World."

At about the time that Japan bombed Pearl Harbor, Albert Einstein wrote to President Franklin D. Roosevelt about the power he theorized could be released from a particle

Churning butter the old way

many scientists said did not even exist—the atom. After letters and conversations with Einstein, the government decided to create a secret facility to test his theory about a powerful bomb being made with atomic energy. Thus, shrouded in a veil of secrecy, a city was born—almost overnight. The families of the small farming community of Bethel Valley were moved, and most of the homes were razed to make way for the Oak Ridge Complex, then called Clinton Engineering Works. The original buildings of the 811-acre complex were built on a 60,000-acre tract of land in a record thirteen months. Production began in 1943.

The U.S. government moved its top scientific minds into the area for what was called the Manhattan Project. It is estimated that houses were constructed every half hour at the height of wartime construction. The secret city reached a peak population of 75,000 and became the fifth-largest city in Tennessee in a little more than two years. By 1945, the entire world knew about Oak Ridge and its research, as Fat Man and Little Boy—the world's first atomic bombs—were dropped on the Japanese cities of Nagasaki and Hiroshima, putting a quick and definite end to World War II.

The gates to the city were finally opened in 1949; today, visitors may tour the area on a thirty-eight-mile Energy/Environment motor loop. Maps of the route are available at the Oak Ridge Welcome Center, at 302 South Tulane Avenue. The loop includes the Graphite Reactor National Historic Site, where visitors may tour the reactor's control room and exhibition areas, featuring original notebooks and gauges that recorded the startup of the world's first functioning reactor. New Bethel Baptist Church, across from the main entrance of Oak Ridge National Laboratory, is also open to the public. Used by scientists for meetings during the war, the church now houses artifacts of the rural life that once thrived here, stories of the relocated families, and images of the construction work that changed the valley.

The entire area of Oak Ridge is on the National Register of Historic Places. One of the best places to learn about the town's history is the American Museum of Science and Energy, at 300 South Tulane Avenue. Most of the bottom floor of the museum is dedicated to the "Oak Ridge Story." To get to that section, visitors have to walk through a wire fence and under a guard tower at a U.S. Checking Station, just like residents of wartime Oak Ridge would have had to do to enter the "Secret City." The exhibit includes a twelve-minute audio-visual presentation, a chronology of the birth of Oak Ridge, and notes from the flight log of the *Enola Gay*, the plane that dropped the atomic bomb on Hiroshima.

Designed for adults and children in the third grade and older, the museum is an entertaining hands-on lesson in science. It includes movies, models, and more than 200 exhibits on everything from nuclear energy to earth energy resources to the automobile to geometry. Kids will be fascinated by the interactive exhibits, computerized displays, and more than thirty computer games. Adults will be amazed at how much things have changed since they last cracked a science book. For instance, there are no longer just three states of matter—solid, liquid, and gas; now there are four—add plasma to the list. And the smallest particle is no longer an atom—it's a quark.

Everyone loves the museum's live demonstrations. The "Static and Dynamic Electricity" demonstration literally made my hair stand on end. If an adult can get a charge out of the live demonstration, imagine the reaction of children.

"When I do these demonstrations, I come away sounding like I know so much," says Judd Brown, exhibit manager for the museum. "So then the kids ask me all kinds of questions, like, 'Is the Starship Enterprise real?' And my favorite question, 'Is the Loch Ness Monster real?' It's great."

Other offerings in the town of Oak Ridge include the Children's Museum (461 West Outer Drive), featuring the region's Appalachian heritage and special programs and displays highlighting art, history, science, and culture from around the world; the Jackson Square Historic Park, located on the original site of Oak Ridge and including some of the original houses; and the University of Tennessee Arboretum (901 Kerr Hollow Road), an educational and research center with more than 800 species of native and exotic plants.

From Oak Ridge, take State 62 to Wartburg, the Morgan County seat. One of the town's biggest attractions is the Obed National Wild and Scenic River, on US 27. A haven for whitewater enthusiasts, the hundred-mile system of rugged waters includes the Obed River, the Emory River, Clear Creek, and Daddy's Creek. *Canoe Magazine* recently listed the Obed River as one of "ten classic rivers" in the United States. The catch is that these rivers are navigable only from about late winter to mid-spring. By early summer, the waterways are reduced to a trickle. *GREY GABLE'S B+B. RUGBY TN.*

From Wartburg, take US 27 north to Elgin and then State 52 west to Rugby. In the late summer, these roads wind past purple and pink wildflowers, cattails, Queen Anne's lace dancing in the fields, and golden sunflowers stretching toward the sky.

Rugby, a British colony founded in 1880, was created as a social experiment by Thomas Hughes, a philanthropist, social reformer, and author of *Tom Brown's School Days.* Hughes wanted to give England's second sons, who did not receive inheritances, a fresh start. Designed as a Utopian society, Rugby was to be the "town of the future." Hughes named it after England's Rugby School, which he attended from 1833 to 1841.

Curious visitors and prospective settlers from all over America and Great Britain came to see what life was like in the new colony. During the 1880s, Rugby was the largest town in three counties, with more than 75 buildings and 450 residents. But then the colonists hit hard times—financial troubles, a typhoid epidemic, and the cruel winters of the Cumberland Plateau. By the turn of the century, the colony had ceased to exist. CLOSED.

Seventeen of the original buildings still stand and are on the National Register of Historic Places; but most are privately owned and are opened only occasionally for Rugby's main events: the Annual Pilgrimage, held in October, and Christmas at Rugby, held in December.

Buildings open throughout the year include the Thomas Hughes Free Public Library, Christ Church Episcopal, Kingstone Lisle (Hughes's own home), and the schoolhouse museum, filled with photographs and memorabilia chronicling Hughes's pursuit of a Utopian society. Visitors may browse through the library as long as they're wearing white gloves kept here just for that purpose. There are copies of the original town newspaper, *The Rugby Gazzette*, and the library's original collection of 7,000 books from American and English publishers. Christ Church Episcopal, which was finished in 1887, stands across the street from the library. It has been a working Episcopal church since 1880, and the original hymnals and prayer books are displayed in glass cases near the entrance. Built of native pine, the small church is adorned with wooden pews, brass and crystal oil lamps, an 1849 rosewood organ, and stained glass widows.

The last stop on the tour is Kingstone Lisle, Hughes's English-style, seven-room rural home, built in 1884 and restored by the Historic Rugby Association in the 1970s. The front parlor of this "bachelor pad" has a piano and plenty of chairs for visitors. The author's original Gothic writing table is in the bedroom, and there are more antiques throughout the house.

While you're in Rugby, you might want to have shepherd's pie at the Harrow Road Cafe, or visit the Rugby Printing Works or the Rugby Commissary. There are several places to stay in town and nearby. The Newbury House, State 52 in Rugby, an authentically restored lodging facility, served as the town's first boardinghouse when it was built in the 1880s. If you're looking for something more modern, try the Grey Gables Bed and Breakfast (on State 52), which was built a few years ago and is operated by Linda and Bill Jones. A charming, two-story gray house, Grey Gables offers eight bedrooms, elegant dinners, and country breakfasts. Dinner is a gourmet affair: ours included cold cucumber soup, spinach and fruit with poppyseed dressing, pork tenderloin, fresh green beans and potatoes "out of Bill's garden," and Bananas Foster for dessert. It was "delish," as one of our tablemates kept exclaiming.

Just a mile or so from Grey Gables on State 52 is Linda Brooks Jones's family emporium, the R. M. Brooks General Store. Listed on the National Register of Historic Places, this old white clapboard structure was built in the 1930s by Linda's grandparents, R. M. and Nettie Brooks. Country general stores are few and far between these days, but fifty years ago they carried everything a family would need—sewing notions, blue-jean overalls, fabric, food, gas, and hardware. You can still find most of those things here, either for sale in the front or on display in the minimuseum in the back of the store. There are old Lance peanut jars, orange Gulf gas pump signs, a George A. Clark thread cabinet, rocking chairs, a potbellied stove, and an old "icy ball."

When Bill Jones's brother-in-law bought the old-fashioned ice maker, neither of them knew what it was. "We just set it up in the store," he says. "And one day, a ninety-year-old man came in and said, 'Why, there's an old icy ball. I haven't seen one of them in years. We used to drive twenty miles in a horse and buggy just to get one ice cube.'"

People visit the store now to buy standard items such as cake mix or soap or candy or to get a slab of old-fashioned cheese. Plenty of people come just to pick up their mail from the little U. S. post office box that sits just inside the front of the store. Linda Jones's mother, Verda Brooks, sorts mail every day in the more than 100-year-old wood-paneled mail room that served as the original Rugby post office. The tiny building was eventually moved into the store. She makes twenty-four cents an hour handling mail for some seventy-five people. "They were going to close the Rugby post office back in 1957 and a lot of these people didn't want to lose their Rugby postmark," says Bill Jones. "So they appealed to then Senator Howard Baker and got to keep a rural post office here—in the store."

Heading west on State 52 toward Allardt, you'll see an entrance to the Big South Fork National River and Recreation Area. Ideal for fishing, horseback riding, hunting, camping, hiking, and canoeing, Big South Fork is one of Tennessee's best-kept secrets. Charit Creek Lodge, the park's backcountry lodging facility, offers rustic log cabins, wood-burning stoves, kerosene lamps, wool blankets, good breakfasts and dinners, and lots of nature. It's a wonderful place to get back to the basics.

Jonathan Blevins, a hunter, built the first cabin at Charit Creek in 1817. Other cabins were built over the years for hunting. Located in four Tennessee counties and one Kentucky county, Big South Fork offers 100,000 acres on the Cumberland Plateau, with 150 miles of hiking trails and 130 miles of horseback riding trails. The park gets its name from the Big South Fork of the Cumberland River, which has carved a gorge into the sandstone plateau, creating sheer cliffs, narrow ridges, and steep-sided gorges. Some of the park's most enchanting spots are Angel Falls, Honey Creek Overlook, and the Twin Arches—natural sandstone formations that look like enormous McDonald's arches rising into the sky. Hikers into the backcountry will see rock "chimney" formations and cascading waterfalls.

Bandy Creek Horse Stables offers guided horseback riding packages that include breakfast, dinner, and an overnight stay at the lodge. Visitors may also tour the park via plane or train. Big South Fork Aero offers a bird's-eye view; Big South Fork Scenic Railway offers scenic train rides through the park.

As if one big, beautiful park weren't enough, the Colditz Cove State Natural Area is just next door—one mile east of Allardt on State 52. The Colditz Cove trail is a small hike with a big payoff. The easy one-mile trail, lined with huge hemlock trees over a hundred years old, as well as mountain laurel and rhododendron, leads to a dancing sixty-foot waterfall called Northrup Falls.

Besides hiking trails, the thirteen miles of State 52 between Rugby and Allardt are dotted with farms and black Angus cows. If you're traveling in September, you're also likely to spot a few *big* pumpkins in the gardens. Allardt is the site of the World Pumpkin Weigh-off, held the first weekend in October. People come from miles around to enter their prize pumpkins in the weigh-off: we're talking orange vegetables that weigh upwards of 800 pounds.

Although there are weigh-offs in other parts of the United States and in Canada that same weekend, Allardt is the only town in the Southeast to host the event. "We were chosen because Jim Asberry, one of our local residents, grew a giant pumpkin (716 pounds plus) that broke the state record and came very shy of being a world record," explains Pat Bryant, a volunteer librarian for Allardt. "There's not a lot of money in the contest. But people compete just for the bragging rights. And if you have the biggest pumpkin, it'll have several hundred seeds. You can sell those for about $1 each."

To grow a *very large* pumpkin, you start out with "giant-type pumpkin seeds," use a lot of fertilizer, and give it a whole lot of tender loving care, Bryant says. "Everybody has their own secrets. You'd be surprised. People really keep their pumpkins hidden. One man who built a small shack around his pumpkin says he guards it with a machine gun. And when the circus was here, you should have seen everyone scrambling to get the elephant fertilizer. They figured it had to be better than cow fertilizer."

Allardt hosts a pumpkin festival in conjunction with the weigh-off, which attracts people from across the United States. The fest includes food, crafts, music, a pumpkin bake-off, a knife and gun show, an antique car show, and a barbecue.

Allardt was established in the 1800s, mostly by German settlers. One of the first settlers to this town of about 700 people was Bruno Gernt. His old office, on Michigan Avenue, and his home, on Baseline Road, both more than a hundred years old, are listed on the National Register of Historic Places. The nineteenth-century home place, which is actually an old restored farmhouse with weather boarding, four bedrooms, and a full kitchen, now serves as an overnight lodge for guests. Rented out by the Gernts, the home place sleeps eight people comfortably.

Jamestown, the Fentress County seat, is about five miles west of Allardt on State 52, at the intersection of US 127. The town was named for James Fentress, a legislator who introduced the bill to create the county, which was established in 1823.

One look around Jamestown and you might think that Mark Twain lived and died here. There's a Mark Twain Apparel, a Mark Twain Inn and Restaurant, and a Mark Twain Park, all on US 127 along the main strip of town. As the story goes, Mark Twain's parents, the Clemenses, were prominent settlers of Jamestown. Mr. Clemens helped design the courthouse and the jail and served as judge. But the couple moved to Missouri six months before little Samuel Langhorne Clemens, otherwise known as Mark Twain, was born. So the

Twain tie-in is that the author of *Tom Sawyer* fame was most likely and very probably conceived here.

The Mark Twain Park, on US 127 is a small, pleasant place with benches and weeping willows. Designated by a historical marker, the park contains a ten-foot wooden bust of the author, which was created by Jamestown's Robert C. Slaven. Jamestown's low buildings and courthouse, made of reddish sandstone, look as though they belong in a west Texas town; you can almost see a Texas flag flying over the courthouse. The town has a laid-back feel—lots of smiling people in pickup trucks with dogs in the back.

For an interesting detour, take US 127 north out of Jamestown about twelve miles to Pall Mall, home of World War I hero Sgt. Alvin C. York. The Fentress County native was born in 1887 in a one-room log cabin near Pall Mall, which was then called Three Forks of the Wolf River. During World War I, York was called to fight—a concept he struggled with. At the age of twenty-eight, he had "gotten saved," and he repudiated war and killing. In the end, however, he decided that it would be better to kill "few" to save "many," so he joined the fight and became one of the most decorated soldiers in American history. At one point, he is said to have shot about thirty German soldiers and captured another hundred soldiers—all single-handedly.

After the war, York and his wife, Gracie, set up a gristmill and store in Pall Mall; both are open for tours. The hero's grave is nearby in an attractive country cemetery that looks off to the hills. The tombstone is marked by an American flag.

Back in Jamestown, take US 127 south to the oldest winery in Tennessee. The Highland Manor Winery offers tours, tastings, and some of the finest Tennessee wine. The English Tudor structure is small and unassuming, but don't be fooled.

There are long waiting lists to purchase several of their products, including the champagne and their Muscadine wine. One teasing taste of the Muscadine and we signed up to buy a bottle—in two years.

Founded thirteen years ago by Irving Martin, the winery sells 60,000 to 65,000 bottles of wine and champagne a year. Tennessee wineries have to grow 20 percent of their grapes; the remainder can come from elsewhere. The Highland Manor Winery harvests four acres of grapes on its property and thirteen acres of grapes in Gallatin, Tennessee. "Our most popular wine is the Highland White," says Debbie Slaven, who works at the winery. "A lot of people like Tennessee wines better because they like them sweet. We have lots of California people come in to buy the wine because they want something different from their typical dry wine."

In the Area

Allardt City Hall (Allardt): 615-879-7125

American Museum of Science and Energy (Oak Ridge): 615-576-3200

Bandy Creek Horse Stables (Big South Fork area): 615-879-4013

Big South Fork National River and Recreation Area: 615-879-3625

Blount Mansion (Knoxville): 615-525-2375

R. M. Brooks General Store (Rugby): 615-628-2533

Charit Creek Lodge (Big South Fork area): 615-429-5704

Children's Museum (Oak Ridge): 615-482-1074

Gernt Home Place (Allardt): 615-879-8517

Grey Gables Bed and Breakfast (Rugby): 615-628-5252

Highland Manor Winery (Jamestown): 615-879-9519

Historic Rugby (Rugby): 615-628-2441

Ijams Nature Center (Knoxville): 615-577-4717

Knoxville Chamber of Commerce (Knoxville): 615-523-7263

Knoxville Museum of Art (Knoxville): 615-525-6101

Knoxville Zoological Park (Knoxville): 615-637-5331

Frank H. McClung Museum (Knoxville): 615-974-2144

Museum of Appalachia (Norris): 615-494-8957

Oak Ridge Convention & Visitors Bureau (Oak Ridge):
615-482-7821

Obed National Wild and Scenic River (Wartburg):
615-346-6294

John Sevier Home (Knoxville): 615-573-5508

Sunsphere (Knoxville): 615-523-4227

Tennessee Theatre (Knoxville): 615-525-1840

University of Tennessee (Knoxville): 615-974-1000

University of Tennessee Arboretum (Oak Ridge):
615-483-3571

James White Fort (Knoxville): 615-525-6514

Sgt. Alvin C. York State Historic Area (Pall Mall):
615-879-9448

4 ~

Sevierville

to

Rutledge

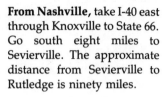

From Nashville, take I-40 east through Knoxville to State 66. Go south eight miles to Sevierville. The approximate distance from Sevierville to Rutledge is ninety miles.

Highlights: *Harrisburg Covered Bridge near Sevierville, fresh-fried apple pies at Kyle Carver Orchards, Grandma's House Bed and Breakfast in Kodak, the bronze statue of Dolly Parton in Sevierville, Mt. Le Conte Lodge, and the wonder of the Great Smoky Mountains.*

Sevierville is a little town with a *big* problem—traffic. Sitting at the crossroads of five major highways, Sevierville sees an average of 54,210 cars travel daily through its main intersection. That's tons of traffic for a town of 7,000 people. For folks on their way to Pigeon Forge and Gatlinburg, Sevierville's just a glimpse—a long glimpse depending upon the traffic. But for those who care to stop, Sevierville is a treasure.

The town was named for John Sevier, who served as the first governor of Tennessee after it was admitted as the sixteenth state of the Union in 1796. The first thing you notice about the town is the Sevier County Courthouse. From any of the congested highways, you can see the Victorian red brick building with its shiny gold domes and bell tower reaching to the sky. Built between 1895 and 1896, the courthouse is topped by a traditional Seth Thomas clock that still chimes on the half hour.

In front of the courthouse, which is on Bruce Street, you'll find a familiar face—a likeness of Dolly Parton. The life-size bronze replica of the Sevierville native was designed by Jim Gray and erected by Dolly fans and friends in 1986. The forty-seven-year-old singer-actress, who shared a three-room cabin with her eleven brothers and sisters while growing up in these parts, is captured playing a guitar while sitting on a rock.

Parton has had quite an impact on the area, bringing a wealth of tourists to Dollywood, a theme park she opened south of town in 1986. She also established a program that awards high school students money for good grades and school participation. In 1991, the blonde beauty was awarded an honorary doctorate from Carson-Newman College in Jefferson City for her personal and professional contributions to the area.

For an interesting detour before heading south from the Sevierville area, go admire the Harrisburg covered bridge, one of four in the state. To reach it, take US 411 east out of Sevierville. Turn right onto State 339 east, also called the Old Newport Highway. Go left at the first junction and then turn right onto Harrisburg Road. The bridge was built in 1875 by Elbert Stephenson Early, a noted bridge builder from Virginia; the structure is registered with the National Historic Society. Supported by "Queenpost" hardwood, the span extends sixty feet across the Little East Fork of the Pigeon River. Inside the one-lane bridge you can look down between wooden support beams and see the babbling brook below. Clapboard siding and a tin roof complete the rustic look of the bridge, which has served as a hiding place for young lovers for more than a hundred years. In the days of horse-drawn buggies, couples would linger under the wooden beams in the darkness and kiss to their hearts' delight.

From Sevierville, head south on US 441, a four-lane highway bordered by open fields and farms. After about seven miles, you'll come to Pigeon Forge—a tourist's dream. A mecca of antique malls, souvenir spots, putt-putt golf courses, an Elvis museum, fast food, and four major outlet malls, Pigeon Forge draws more than seven million tourists annually.

Driving more than two miles an hour along US 441 is at times impossible, especially in the fall when you're sharing the road with University of Tennessee football fans, car show patrons, shoppers, craft fair enthusiasts, and tourists on their way to the Dollywood amusement park or the Smoky Mountains.

One of the fastest ways out of town is by air. You can hop a ride on a helicopter and skim the tops of the majestic Smoky Mountains. You can also try bungee jumping seventy-five feet from a crane, which may lead to the second fastest way out of town—by ambulance.

From Pigeon Forge it's just a hop, skip, and jump to Gatlinburg. At least 80 percent of Gatlinburg's tourists are repeats coming to see the splendor of the Smoky Mountains, to visit the gift shops, and to get married. Yes, Gatlinburg has been called the marriage capital of the world. There are five wedding chapels, some of which handle up to thirty weddings a day. It's a honeymooner's paradise, with chalets, hotels, and lots of attractions. Gatlinburg can accommodate up to 35,000 guests a night, a startling number considering that the town's population is just under 3,500.

Hiking the Great Smoky Mountains

Driving through Gatlinburg on US 441, a four-lane road where the pedestrian has the right-of-way, is no easy trek. But the slow pace gives visitors a chance to see what the town at the foot of the hills has to offer—attractions such as the Smoky Mountain Winery, Ober Gatlinburg recreation park, the Mountain Mall, Hillbilly Golf, and the Gatlinburg Sky Lift. If you plan to see the sights of Gatlinburg, take the trolley. It's much faster than a car.

A visit to this mountain town can be very enlightening (excuse the pun), especially around Christmas. More than two million "Smoky Mountain Lights" are lit for the occasion, turning the town into an enchanting fantasyland. Lights form chandelier-like arches over The Parkway, Gatlinburg's main street, and create three-dimensional bell towers rising twenty-eight feet into the mountain skies.

If you want to get away from the bright lights and big city, head for the hills, er, mountains. More than nine million people annually visit the Great Smoky Mountains, the most visited national park in the United States. From US 441, take Cherokee Orchard Road into the park, a sanctuary to more than 1,500 different kinds of flowering plants and more varieties of trees than in all of Europe. The Great Smoky Mountains National Park is the largest deciduous forest in the United States. The park was created in 1934; the mountains, whose highest peaks reach 6,000 feet, get their name from the smokelike haze that envelops them.

Cherokee Orchard Road winds around Piney Mountain, crosses over brooks, passes antiquated cabins, and offers plenty of picture-perfect views. Call ahead if you're traveling in the winter. The park closes some of the roads when weather conditions make them impassable.

If you love nature, it doesn't get any better than this: 800 square miles of wildlife. The Smokies are a great getaway any time of the year for camping, hiking, and seeing wildlife.

Smoky Mountains National Park has a large collection of historic buildings—century-old gristmills that still grind corn, barns that still house livestock, and log cabins built by the farmers who scraped a living out of these mountains a hundred years ago.

Along the park's 800 miles of maintained hiking trails, visitors may spot deer, red wolves (which have been released in the park on an experimental basis), all kinds of birds, squirrels, river otters, salamanders (there are twenty-six known species in the park), and black bears. The park even has its share of llamas. Originally from the Andes Mountains, the gray-and-white llamas can be seen on the trails three times a week carrying fresh vegetables, fruit, and clean linen up to the folks at Mt. Le Conte Lodge, situated on the third highest peak in the park, about 5,900 feet above sea level. The lodge used to employ horses for transporting, but now llamas do the work because their padded feet don't damage the trails.

Open from late March to mid-November, the lodge accommodates up to fifty people. Making a reservation can be as difficult as getting front row tickets to a Los Angeles Lakers home game, but it's sure worth the wait. At the top of the mountain, campers swap stories of how many consecutive weeks they called just trying to get through to the reservation desk. People *do* clamor for a chance to spend the day hiking to a cabin with no electricity, telephone, or running water. Part of Le Conte's appeal is that it's the only lodging facility in the Smoky Mountains and the only hiking lodge in the southeastern United States. Forty to 60 percent of the Le Conte lodge guests come back at least once, if not annually. We made the hike in November, on the last weekend the lodge was open, and the coldest of the year—only twelve degrees. It was the kind of cold where you don't mind resting your feet directly *on* the kerosene heaters, and at night you wonder why seven wool blankets feel like one cotton sheet.

Five muscle-straining trails lead up to the lodge. They range in distance from five to eight miles and include The Boulevard, Alum Cave, Trillium Gap, Bullhead, and Rainbow Falls trails. We climbed Trillium Gap, which begins on Cherokee Orchard Road, also known as the Roaring Fork Motor Nature Trail. The trailhead is less than ten miles from Gatlinburg. Plenty of people hike the first mile or so of this trail to see Grotto Falls, a cascade that has carved its niche into the side of the mountain. Hikers actually have to pass under the waterfall to continue on Trillium Gap Trail, a 6.5-mile path that climbs in and around several arms of the mountain.

The hardest part of the trail, which takes the average hiker five hours to climb, comes right after Grotto Falls, where the trail becomes increasingly steep. Along the trail, which climbs 3,300 feet in elevation, you'll feel the crunching of leaves beneath your feet, hear the rustle of animals moving in the trees around you, and see some incredible views. You'll also seem to be climbing forever. Then, just when you've asked for the 129th time, "How much farther?" you'll see a cluster of gray cabins and people shuffling around. In the main lodge, there's an endless supply of steamy homemade hot chocolate and plenty of folks to meet.

Dinner is served at 6:00 P.M. We're not talking canned chicken and trail mix. The hearty repast usually includes three vegetables, a roast or chicken 'n dumplings, corn bread, fruit, coffee, hot chocolate, and dessert—all homemade. Wine is even served if you order ahead. After dinner, guests gather in the lodge to sing, play guitar, talk, or play one of the many games the lodge has on hand. You can also gaze at the stars or look down a "million miles" below at the twinkling lights of Gatlinburg. Most people turn in early up here—a long day's hike and lots of nature can wear you out.

Breakfast is at 8:00 A.M. and then it's back down the mountain. Ordinarily going down is a lot easier than climbing up, but the twelve-degree weather during our visit had turned the paths into sheets of ice. On the way down the mountain, we passed the llamas, bringing up the last load of linens. It's a good thing the place was closing for the season: the llamas didn't look as though they enjoyed the ice any more than we did.

If you plan to hike, camp, or drive through the Smoky Mountains, you'll need a map of the trails. For information and park maps, visit the Sugarlands Visitor Center, which is located at the intersection of Newfound Gap and Little River roads inside the park.

Follow Cherokee Orchard Road out of the park and go east on US 321, which takes you through the mountains and into glorious valleys, flanked on either side by open pastures. Along the way, you'll see a number of arts and crafts shops set up in people's homes, advertising wood crafts, quilts, and other handmade items.

After about twenty miles, US 321 descends into Cosby, an unincorporated town where you'll see country homes, the Lit'l Creek Restaurant and Music Bar, Cosby Barbecue Pit, and a shooting range. You'd better be a good shot though: the range runs parallel to the road—and moving cars.

Not too long ago, you could also whistle up some illicit whiskey in the area. "At one time Cosby was the moonshine capital of the world," says Pauline Shields Walker, eighty-nine, who grew up in town. "Those days were so long ago. Cosby was an isolated part of Cocke County. The only way to make a living was to turn corn to whiskey; it was much easier to transport that way. The only thing that was wrong with it was it was illegal."

Dr. E. P. Muncy, the Jefferson County historian, used to own a seventy-acre farm in Cosby. One time, the retired physician startled a group of people while walking near a creek on his property. "I came down the mountain and everyone ran off," Muncy said of the moonshiners. "They left a still behind. The one old man who stayed came up to me and told me why the others had run off. So I asked why he had stayed. He said, 'I haven't seen a revenuer come off the mountain yet waving his arms.' "

From Cosby, take State 32 north toward Newport. Look around and see the brilliant hues of the Blue Ridge Mountains. Along this route you'll see many signs for apples, one of the biggest cash crops in the area. If you're an apple aficionado, stop in at Kyle Carver Orchards, in business for forty years selling all kinds of apple products, such as apple jelly, cider, and butter, from apples grown on their property. In the warehouse, you can buy other things too, such as fresh potatoes, nuts, fruit jams, pumpkin butter, sweet pepper jelly, apple relish, and taffy. Whether you're hungry or not, there's an apple sorter to watch in action. I highly recommend the fresh-fried warm apple pies.

All along State 32, Black Angus and Hereford cows graze in the shadows of the Blue Ridge Mountains, and tall trees wave their puffs of orange, cinnamon, and maroon fall foliage to the sky. Besides big open pastures, the two-lane road has a church about every four miles.

In Newport, the Cocke County seat, you'll see Victorian homes, the Newport Speedway, lots of strip malls, and the Woodzo Drive-In movie theater. The drive-in's grass parking area is empty during the day, but you can almost picture the night scene—the caravan of cars and the rush of teenagers eager to turn on their speakers and tune out the movie.

Leave Newport on US 411 west, which passes a flea market, a series of car repair and hot-rodding shops, and homes with shiny red Phillips 66 stock cars parked out back. The two-lane highway winds around extra-sharp curves, passing small houses nestled into the sides of the mountain where the soil is rocky and the grades are steep.

After about five miles of seat-clutching curves, you come to Chestnut Hill, an unincorporated town with no more than 3,000 residents. The main business in the area is Bush's Canned Foods, which employs 350 people. As the story goes, A. J. Bush was a schoolteacher and a general store owner who founded A. J. Bush and Company in 1907 to provide jobs in the area. What started out as a "small potatoes" tomato-processing plant has become a major operation, canning more than 75 percent of the country's vegetables. The Bush family also owns the bank and the General Merchant's Store, which sells "just about everything."

From Chestnut Hill, turn right onto State 92 north, a two-lane road leading into Dandridge, one of the oldest cities in the state, and the Jefferson County seat. Settlers traveling the Holston and the French Broad rivers by boat stumbled upon the area of Jefferson County around 1783. By 1788, pioneers such as Adam Peck and Adam Meek were moving in.

Dandridge, named for Martha Dandridge Washington, wife of the country's first president, was established in 1793. The city's streets are lined with thirty well-preserved Victorian homes—some of which house businesses—all on the National Register of Historic Places. The Greek Revival-style Jefferson County Courthouse, built around 1845, is the oldest courthouse still in use in the state. It also houses the Jefferson County Museum, where you can see Civil War relics, a feather-trimmed folding fan from the 1800s, and the original marriage bond of David Crockett and Polly Finley.

From Dandridge, continue north on State 92 to Jefferson City. The four-lane flat expanse of road passes fast-food places such as McDonald's and Burger King, sure to jolt you back into the twentieth century. Back before the Quarter Pounder, this town was known as Mossy Creek and at one time was part of North Carolina. Jefferson City was settled in

1783 and named after the third president of the United States, Thomas Jefferson.

Today it's a college town. Carson Newman College, with its red brick buildings, originally opened in 1851 as the Mossy Creek College. It later became Carson College for men and in 1889 joined with nearby Newman College for women. Today, more than 2,000 students attend the coed liberal arts institution.

Before leaving town, be sure to visit the Glenmore Mansion, at 1280 North Chucky Pike. Built in 1869 by Col. John Roper Branner, who was president of what eventually became the Southern Railroad, the five-story mansion is considered to be an almost perfect example of Victorian architecture. Originally known as The Oaks, the building has twenty-seven rooms, eight of which are open to the public.

If you have time, continue north on State 92 to Rutledge. You'll pass the Cherokee Dam Tennessee Valley Authority Reservation and Cherokee Lake, as well as quarter horses, cattle, and barns bursting at the seams with drying tobacco in the fall.

Nestled in the foothills of the mountains, Rutledge is the Grainger County seat. Here, you'll find the Old Grainger County Jail, the oldest brick jailhouse in Tennessee. Built in 1848, the jail was restored by the county's historical society. You won't find any criminals here now—it's a meeting hall for area clubs and organizations.

If you're looking for a place to stay, there's a good bed and breakfast near the beginning of the trip. On the northwestern outskirts of Kodak, which is about eight miles north of Sevierville, is Grandma's House, at 734 Pollard Road. To get there, take State 92 from Rutledge to Jefferson City. Then go west on US 11E to State 139. Go south on State 139 to Kodak. Started in 1990, the bed and breakfast offers lazy days, friendly conversation, and belt-loosening breakfasts. The two-story white Colonial home is twenty-five miles from Gatlinburg and fifteen miles from Knoxville. Run by Charlie and Hilda Hickman, Grandma's House can sleep up to eight people. They leave the light on if you're running late, and they'll even come and get you if you're lost.

The bed and breakfast is open year-round; during the winter months, Grandma's House offers an intriguing attraction—murder mystery weekends. Groups of six to eight people participate in "Death by Design" whodunits written by Hilda. "No one's figured out the killer yet," says Hilda. "Not even a former New York police detective who came to visit us."

In the Area

Dollywood (Pigeon Forge): 615-428-9486

Gatlinburg Chamber of Commerce (Gatlinburg): 800-568-4748

Glenmore Mansion (Jefferson City): 615-475-7643

Grandma's House (Kodak): 615-933-3512, 800-676-3512

Great Smoky Mountains National Park: 615-436-1200

Jefferson County Museum (Dandridge): 615-397-3800

Kyle Carver Orchards (Newport): 615-487-2419

Mt. Le Conte Lodge (Great Smoky Mountains National Park): 615-429-5704

Pigeon Forge Department of Tourism (Pigeon Forge): 800-251-9100

Sevierville Chamber of Commerce (Sevierville): 800-255-6411

5 ~

Dayton

to

Sweetwater

From Nashville, take I-40 east through Knoxville. Take I-75 south approximately fifty-eight miles to State 30. Go west on US 30 approximately twenty-five miles to Dayton. The total trip length from Dayton to Sweetwater is 117 miles.

Highlights: *The Rhea County Courthouse, site of the Scopes Monkey Trial; the wonder of the Cherokee National Forest; the churning rapids of the Ocoee; the largest underwater lake in the world; the history of the Cherokee Indians; the mining area of Ducktown; and the gold diggers of Coker Creek.*

Outside of Dayton, the smell of honeysuckle and freshly tilled soil wafts through the air. In town, people stroll along the square. It's almost dinnertime and the attorneys are just closing their briefcases at the Rhea County Courthouse, a century-old building that has seen its share of trials. One in 1925 seemed a pretty clear-cut case against a man who was teaching evolution. That was against the law in Tennessee.

It all started when John Washington Butler, a farmer and father of five, discovered that his children were learning evolution in school. A Tennessee state legislator, Butler worried that his children might be "corrupted," so he introduced a bill

71

to prohibit the teaching of the theory of evolution. Biology teacher John T. Scopes, twenty-four, agreed to become the defendant in a test case trial for violating a new Tennessee statute making it unlawful "to teach any theory that denies the story of the Divine Creation of man as taught in the Bible." Scopes was represented by Clarence Darrow and Dudley Malone, who were retained by the American Civil Liberties Union. Three-time presidential candidate William Jennings Bryan was the prosecuting attorney.

More than a thousand people came to the trial, an eleven-day "media event" that put Dayton on the map. The history of the trial is memorialized in a minimuseum on the bottom floor of the Rhea County Courthouse. It includes photographs, newspaper articles, and toy monkeys that were sold as trial souvenirs. *The Scopes Trial: Destiny in Dayton* is a play and festival held each year in July. A cast of forty people, with dialogue taken directly from the trial transcript, take visitors back to the gripping trial. Afterward, there's a dinner on the grounds and tours around town in antique cars and horse-drawn wagons.

Dayton's other big annual event is the Tennessee Strawberry Festival. Held the third weekend in May, the fest draws between 80,000 and 90,000 people for country music, arts and crafts, food, sports, a parade, a carnival, and a beauty pageant for children.

You can leave Dayton by car, bus, or boat. Two of the main highways out of town end in water, where ferries take you to the other side. State 30 east leads to the Tennessee River, where the Old Washington Ferry takes you across to Decatur. If you take State 60 south out of Dayton, you'll come to the Blythes Ferry, which crosses the Tennessee River and puts you on your way to Cleveland.

Both of these ferries were at one time owned and operated by the Cherokee Indian Nation. The Old Washington Ferry, which carries 200 cars and trucks a day across the waters of the Tennessee—a few at a time, is the third oldest wooden ferry in the United States. You can hear the ferry putting as it pushes its way against the waves created by the ski and fishing boats that cross its path. State 30, a two-lane farm road that leads to the ferry, passes cows, pastures, and barbecue places. Where the water meets the road there'll be a long line of cars with their engines cut and people standing around talking, reading, drinking sodas, or chewing tobacco. This is what you might call a country traffic jam. If you're behind three or four cars, a tractor, and a semitruck, you might as well sit back and enjoy the big open pastures around you.

Take State 60 south toward Cleveland, the biggest city you'll pass through on this trip, and the Bradley County seat. Be forewarned—it's about the last stop for a quick meal, a large grocery store, and places that accept some kind of payment besides cash. Beyond Cleveland, State 60 is a two-lane road bordered by country homes, ponds, and silos.

About twelve miles south of Cleveland, look hard for signs to the Red Clay State Historic Area (at 1140 Red Clay Park Road), site of one of the saddest chapters in American history. The area marks the beginning of the Trail of Tears—a forced march in 1838 of about 18,000 Cherokee Indians from their native lands east of the Mississippi River. The thousand-mile cross-country march to the Oklahoma Territory was held mostly in midwinter. It was a journey of despair, one the Cherokee called "Nun-da-ut-sun'y," or "The Trail Where They Cried." More than 4,000 people died along the way, nearly one quarter of the Cherokee Nation.

Private John G. Burnett, of the 2nd Tennessee Volunteers, who was assigned to the removal, gave this account: "In the chill of a drizzling rain on an October morning I saw them loaded like cattle or sheep into 645 wagons and started moving toward the west. One can never forget the sadness and solemnity of that morning. Chief John Ross led in prayer and while the bugle was sounded and the wagons started rolling, many of the children rose to their feet and waved their little hands good-bye to their mountain homes, knowing they were leaving them forever."

The Red Clay Museum, which is housed on 275 acres of the original council grounds, doesn't dwell on the awful reality of that journey, but instead celebrates the life of the Cherokee tribe. By the 1830s, many of the Cherokee had adapted to the white man's ways, learning skilled labor, creating their own alphabet, establishing their own constitution and system of government and elections, and publishing a newspaper, *The Phoenix.* Many of the Cherokee became better educated and wealthier than the white men who had forced them off their lands.

The museum's displays focus on everything from the Cherokee Green Corn Dance to religion to Anetsa, a traditional Cherokee ball game. Be sure to tour the reproduction two-story log house, a dwelling typical of a middle-class Cherokee family in the 1800s. The beautifully landscaped park offers hiking trails, bike trails, and picnic areas on land where the Cherokee once lived in peace and prosperity.

Many Native Americans return to the area each year in August to celebrate Cherokee Day of Recognition. The festival includes Native American dancers, traditional arts and crafts, food, and storytelling.

Back in Cleveland, take US 64 east toward Ocoee. If you're interested in Native American history, outside of Cleveland go north on US 411 toward Benton. After about three miles you'll see a historical marker telling about the importance of one Nancy Ward, "beloved woman" of the Overhill Cherokees. A concrete path circles up to the nicely groomed grave of Ward, a princess and prophetess of the Cherokee nation, who was considered the Pocahontas of Tennessee. Ward, who lived from 1738 to 1822, prevented massacres of white settlers and introduced milk cows to the Cherokee economy.

US 64 winds its way through the unincorporated town of Ocoee and becomes a Forest Service Scenic Byway once inside the Cherokee National Forest. Named for the people who cared for the area more than a century ago, Tennessee's only national forest offers opportunities for backpacking, cross-country skiing, fishing, hiking, canoeing, swimming, hunting, and relaxing. About three million people annually visit the forest, whose 625,000 acres hug the Great Smoky Mountains. Pick up a trail map at one of the seven forest service offices. The nearest one to the Ocoee River is the Ocoee Ranger District, fifteen miles east of Cleveland on US 64.

The scenic highway offers the splendor of the Cherokee National Forest on one side and the sparkling waters of the Ocoee River on the other. Visitors fish and swim in some of the calmer areas of the river. Kayakers and whitewater rafters attack the river's tumultuous rapids. Long an international favorite for whitewater enthusiasts, the Ocoee River was chosen to host the whitewater rafting competition during the 1996 Olympics in nearby Atlanta. The Ocoee River's Class IV and V rapids (on a scale from I to VI) make it one of the nation's most challenging rivers.

Twenty-four outfitters offer whitewater rafting trips along the Ocoee River from the third week in March to the end of October. For a list of some of the outfitters, call the Cleveland/Bradley County Chamber of Commerce at (615) 472-6587. The rafting guides give the history of the river and its rapids. This trip is the best way to see the Ocoee flume, one of the oldest wooden flumes in the United States. Listed on the National Register of Historic Places, the flume was built in 1912 by the Tennessee Power Company as a way to generate electricity. The flume—an inclined trough for

Take a ride on the Ocoee River

conveying water—runs along the river for a little more than four miles. At the beginning of the trip, the flume is almost parallel to the river. By the end of the trip, it's about 230 feet above the river. That's because the river drops about 250 feet in elevation during the 5.2-mile raft trip.

From Cherokee National Forest, head east on US 64, and then north on State 68 to Ducktown, which is located in the Copper Basin. Named for Cherokee Chief Duck, whose people had once lived in this valley, Ducktown sprang up with the copper mines in 1851.

The Ducktown Basin Museum, which occupies one of the hilltop buildings of the once prosperous Burra Burra Mine, overlooks the barren hills of the Copper Basin. Listed on the National Register of Historic Places, the museum embraces the town's heritage of copper mining. Copper was discovered here in 1843; by 1855, this area was the nation's leading producer of copper, with more than thirty companies mining beneath the valley's topsoil. The museum features aerial maps, cases of copper mining tools, and a twenty-minute documentary on the history of the area.

To separate copper from zinc, iron, and sulfur, miners had to heat the ore at extremely high temperatures. For this, they created ovens in the earth, digging sometimes 600 feet deep and burning every tree in sight within a fifty-mile radius. Billows of sulfur dioxide gas clouded Ducktown and the surrounding area, eventually creating an acid rain that choked the plants and wildlife in the area.

Dorothy Lashbrook, a guide for the Ducktown Basin Museum, remembers when the mines were still in operation. "We'd walk to school and have to hold our noses to keep the sulfuric acid fumes out," says Lashbrook, who was born in Ducktown in 1916. "We kept the windows closed at school because there was so much sulfur. We couldn't even see across the creek—we'd just have to call to see if our neighbors were ready to walk to school."

In 1987, the 144-year-old mining history of the Copper Basin came to an end with the closing of the last of the modern mining operations. Because of the utter environmental destruction of the area, the Copper Basin is one of the few identifiable interior landmarks from space satellites. Efforts are being made to bring the area back to life with newly planted trees and other vegetation. Yet Ducktown natives, such as Lashbrook, don't look forward to the change. "These hills are our heritage," she says. "I like the bare hills—that's who we are."

From Ducktown, follow State 68 north through Turtletown and Farner toward Coker Creek. When you reach Farner, you'll be in the Cherokee National Forest again and there will be signs for Coker Creek Falls, a beautiful area with fourteen waterfalls. This is a superb place to hike.

Gold was discovered along Coker Creek in 1831; some $80,000 worth of gold was taken from here between 1831 and 1854. Dreamers still pan for gold in the creek. Just about any hour of the day, you'll see people of all ages bent over, dragging pans through the creek's waters, looking for gold. If you forget to bring your pan, you can borrow one from the Old Country Store. If you're lucky, Sanford Gray, who owns the store with his wife, Esther, and who has found "as many as thirty points in one pan," will give you a tip or two on how to strike it rich.

The Old Country Store, built of barn lumber and sitting in the middle of a big grassy field, is a hodgepodge of sewing notions, quilts, antiques, and handmade items from area craftspeople. On Saturday nights, the store's walls ring with the music of local musicians and singers.

In addition to running the store, the Grays organize group camping trips and offer rental places in the area. They also own the Village Inn, the restaurant across the street from the store, which is open weekends. The big, casual, one-room restaurant serves country-style foods, a salad bar, and fantastic fried chicken. The homemade desserts are good, too; be sure to try some of Esther Gray's chocolate meringue pie. The hearty country breakfasts are also wonderful—country fried eggs, ham, bacon, homemade biscuits, pancakes, cereal, and juice.

We spent the night in a little red house owned by the Grays. Cozy, clean, and set in the woods, the rental house slept six people comfortably. It's just up the street from the store, so you're still close to "all the action."

One of the area's biggest events is the Coker Creek Autumn Gold Festival, held the second weekend in October. The festival draws between 2,000 and 5,000 people, "depending on the weather," and includes gold panning, arts and crafts, nature hikes, covered wagon rides, syrup making, board splitting, clogging, and country music.

From Coker Creek, take State 68 north to Madisonville, then US 411 east to Vonore. The two-lane road passes through small communities with flea markets, churches, small stores, and family-owned businesses. Vonore is home of the Sequoyah Birthplace Museum, the only Native American, tribally owned museum in the country. Located on Citico Road, on the banks of Tellico Lake on Cherokee tribal land, the museum honors Sequoyah, a soldier and statesman who worked for twelve years creating the Cherokee alphabet. The only man in history to single-handedly develop and perfect an alphabet, Sequoyah presented his work to the Cherokee people in 1821. Today he is remembered as one of the greatest of all Cherokee Indians.

Opened in 1986, the museum includes a large-scale rendering of Sequoyah's syllabary, an audio recording of how each of the symbols is pronounced, and a display of artifacts dating back to 7300 B.C.

Return to State 68 going north toward Sweetwater, and look for signs for the Lost Sea, "the largest underground lake in the world," according to the *Guinness Book of World Records*. Actually part of the Craighead Caverns, the Lost Sea is a four-and-a-half-acre subterranean lake. The one-hour tour takes visitors through several cave chambers and includes almost a mile of walking in the cave, which is fifty-eight degrees year-round.

Craighead Caverns has been used by lots of different people. The Cherokee Indians met in one of the chambers, which is now called "The Council Room." During the Civil War, the Confederate army mined the cave for saltpeter, which was used to make gunpowder. One of the chambers served as a dance hall for a short period. You'll see moonshine stills at different points in the cave. Another room contains an enormous supply of rations, some say put there during the cold war paranoia of the 1950s. The earliest known visitor to the cave, however, was a giant Pleistocene-era jaguar that wandered into the cave 20,000 years ago. Its tracks can be found in the deepest part of the cave; its bones, found in 1939, are now on display in the American Museum of Natural History in New York City.

Opened in 1964 as a museum, the cave features stalagmites, stalactites, hanging rock, bedrock, and an abundance of crystalline rock formations known as anthodites. Because the fragile, spiky formations are so rare, the Lost Sea is designated as a Registered Natural Landmark.

The Lost Sea itself, which is at the bottom of the cave, was discovered in 1905 by a thirteen-year-old boy named Ben Sands. Exploring, the teenager wiggled through a tiny opening and found himself in a huge room filled with water. He threw mudballs as far as he could into the blackness in every direction and heard nothing but splashes.

Today, visitors don't have to throw mudballs to see that the body of water is *huge*. They can experience its vastness during a short ride in a glass-bottomed boat powered by an electric motor. Underwater lights, pockets of darkness, shadows, and abnormally large rainbow trout give the lake an eerie feel. The fish were originally put in the lake to see if there were any other exits; so far none have been found. Or else the fish know a way out, but stay here because where else are they going to be fed handfuls of Purina Trout Chow every twenty minutes or so by guests and guides?

80

In the Area

Cherokee National Forest: 615-476-9700

Cleveland/Bradley County Chamber of Commerce
(Cleveland): 615-472-6587

Coker Creek Village (Coker Creek): 615-261-2310

Dayton/Rhea County Chamber of Commerce: 615-775-0361

Ducktown Basin Museum (Ducktown): 615-496-5778

Lost Sea (Sweetwater): 615-337-6616

Ocoee Ranger District, Cherokee National Forest
(Cleveland): 615-338-5201

Red Clay State Historic Area and Museum (Cleveland):
615-478-0339

Sequoyah Birthplace Museum (Vonore): 615-884-6246

Tennessee Department of Environment and Conservation:
615-338-4133

Wildwater Limited: 800-451-9972

HISTORICAL MARKER- NANCY WARD.
PROUD CHEROKEE WOMAN.

6 ~

Lafayette

to

Cookeville

From Nashville, take I-65 north approximately ten miles to State 174. Take State 174 east approximately fifteen miles to Gallatin. From Gallatin, take State 25 east eleven miles. When State 25 intersects US 231, continue east on State 10. Go east on State 10 approximately twelve miles to Lafayette. The total trip length from Lafayette to Cookeville is seventy-six miles.

Highlights: *The whittlers of Lafayette; the history and mineral water of Red Boiling Springs; Clorina Andrews's brown sugar pie; the troughs of trout at the Dale Hollow National Fish Hatchery; and the Cookeville Depot Museum in Cookeville.*

One of the main attractions of Lafayette can be found just about any day under the shade of an old oak tree on the south side of the town's public square. That's where members of the Spit and Whittle Gang gather to enjoy the breeze, trade knives, swap stories, and talk politics. This handful of mostly retired men also whittles. Anyone's welcome to sit a spell on one of the long benches, says Henry Gammons, a native of Lafayette.

"You wouldn't believe all the people who come out here," says Gammons. "People come all the time. These two women from California were out here whittling with us last week."

Gammons, who retired last September, wasn't whittling the Saturday we visited. "That's work and I quit work last year."

They're an entertaining lot, laughing and talking. And they don't mind answering questions about directions, local politics, or where the fish are biting. I asked them if there was anything else to do in the town. Gammons looked at his buddies and said, "No, we're about it."

Well, there *are* a few other things to see in Lafayette, which is the Macon County seat. There's the stately Macon County Courthouse, at the center of town. The county, established in 1843, is named for North Carolina statesman Nathaniel Macon.

There's also the Lafayette Key Park / Log House at 208 Church Street. The small structure was the second house built in Macon County when it was constructed in 1824. The historic dwelling today serves as the home of the Macon County Historical Society and sits in the middle of a four-acre park.

From Lafayette, take State 52 east toward Red Boiling Springs. Black wood fences, winding roads, and towering green fields of tobacco make this a pleasant drive.

Kentucky pioneers seeking greener pastures in Tennessee settled in Red Boiling Springs around the middle of the nineteenth century. Edmund Jennings, a Kentucky hunter, was reportedly among the first of the settlers. The hunter followed an animal trail that led to a salt lick, the head of Salt Lick Creek.

Shepherd Kirby, of Kentucky, was one of the throngs of people who moved to the area, then called Salt Lick. As the story goes, Kirby had suffered for years with a serious eye infection. One day while he was hewing logs to build a home, his eyes started burning, so he went to a nearby spring to bathe them. The cool water helped, and he continued to come to the spring until his eye disorder remarkably vanished. News of the healing spread like kudzu and pretty soon people were coming from near and far to the town's springs to be cured of every imaginable illness. About this time, a spring with red-tinted water was discovered coming out of the ground, so the community's name was changed to Red Boiling Springs.

The town's first hotel, The Deadman Hotel, was supposedly built around 1860. By 1918, there were four hotels. Throngs of visitors, including vacationers and people seeking cures, would come and stay in Red Boiling Springs for weeks and months at a time. The town hit its heyday in the 1920s, adding four more hotels and at least a dozen boardinghouses. Still there wasn't enough room for all the visitors.

People came for the picnics, barbecues, bowling alleys, tennis, and, of course, the mineral water. At the time, there were five different types of mineral water—red, black, white, freestone, and double and twist. They got their names from the colors each water would turn a silver coin, except for double and twist, which supposedly got its name from a person's physical reaction after tasting the stuff.

Nestled in the foothills of the Cumberland Mountains, the historic community of Red Boiling Springs still has three of its original hotels, built around the turn of the century. The Cloyd Hotel, Armour's Red Boiling Springs Hotel, and the Donoho Hotel are still in operation today.

A visit to the Donoho Hotel is literally a step back into the past. Built in 1914, the hotel, at 500 East Main Street, is a large, white, two-story wood structure with more than fifty rooms, a gift shop, a music room with a piano and TV, and an old-fashioned dining room. The guest rooms are clean and simple—a double bed and private bath with a shower. No frills, no fuss, and no central heating or air-conditioning. Fans in the summer and blankets in the winter keep the lodgers who flock to the hideaway year-round comfortable.

People come here for the slow pace, peaceful atmosphere, and good southern cooking, including a big country breakfast, ample lunch, and huge dinner. A dinner bell rings before meals, letting everyone know it's time to loosen their belt. For dinner, cured ham, potatoes, fried chicken, green beans, cooked apples, hot biscuits, and homemade preserves are brought out steaming to the big, family-style tables. The bottomless serving bowls keep on coming. When you think you couldn't lift your fork one more time, dessert appears.

After dinner, most people head for the rows of well-worn rocking chairs on the porches, which run the length of the top and bottom floors. It's a great place for reading, talking, and watching fireflies. "There's not a lot to do down here," says Jeff Cowden, who owns the hotel with his wife, Talisa. "We watch the traffic light change. Of course it just blinks yellow."

Talisa asks a guest if she enjoyed her dinner conversation, and the woman smiles and says yes. "Good," Talisa says. "That's our main entertainment around here."

The Cowdens, originally from Nashville, saw the Donoho Hotel for the first time about a year ago when they came to town to help their cousins restore the Cloyd Hotel, which is now called the Thomas House. "My wife came down here for a Coke and we bought the hotel," Jeff says. "It was the most expensive Coke I ever bought."

When we visited, the Cowdens were working night and day refurbishing the rooms. "This is such a neat change from Nashville," Talisa says. "It's like a storybook place. We hope it never changes. We've made some of the greatest friends since we've been here. And you can hardly get any work done during the day for all the people who want to come and talk to you and tell you about all the dances and social events they attended at this hotel."

The Cowdens and their two teenage children enjoy all of the guests—even the uninvited ones, such as Gretta, the friendly ghost. "This house is full of history," Talisa explains. "There used to be lots of dancing and laughter, and people would drive from miles around to come here. And when we hear Gretta, we normally hear big band music and happy chatter.

"Don't worry, she doesn't stay in a rented room," Talisa says to one big-eyed guest. "She stays in a storage room and she seems happy. This place has always been a happy place— a place where friendships are made."

Besides rocking chairs and fresh air, the hotel also has a volleyball net, a badminton set, horseshoes, and a park nearby for the kiddies. Within walking distance of the hotel are two picturesque covered bridges, made of barn lumber, built in the 1970s. One is on Church Street and the other is on Valley View.

Palace Park, off State 52, also offers several sulfur wells where people can taste the "healing" water. Or you might want to go for a mineral bath at the nearby Armour's Red Boiling Springs Hotel, at 321 East Main Street. Built in 1924, the two-story brick hotel is on the National Register of Historic Places and has the only operating mineral bathhouse in the state.

A mineral bath begins with a ten-minute sitz bath in an antique claw-foot tub. This is a wear-your-bathing-suit kind of thing, but not your best bathing suit, because the sulfur water in the tub is *black*. If you can get over the fact that you can't see your legs and feet underwater, and if you like the smell of rotten eggs, you'll do just fine.

After the bath, you step into a small, steam-filled sauna. Next stop is the "sweat cot," a heated cot with fresh white linens. Then you get a lotion rubdown. The whole experience is interesting and funny and reportedly therapeutic.

The annual Red Boiling Springs Folk Medicine Festival draws some 5,000 people to the area each July. Although the emphasis is on medicinal herbs and holistic medicine, there are also children's rides, live music, a talent show, concessions, homemade ice cream, and crafts and booths of Native American wares.

From Red Boiling Springs, take State 52 east. The road zigs and zags through captivating countryside, with valleys stretching off both sides of the road. Outside of Moss, the road climbs along a ridge, flanked by deep, wild hollows of forests. The Clay County Veterans Memorial Bridge crosses over the Cumberland River and into Celina, the Clay County seat. Established in 1870, the town of 1,600 people was named for Celina Fisk, daughter of pioneer educator Moses Fisk.

The Clay County Courthouse, which was built in 1872, serves as the focal point of the square. On the National Register of Historic Places, the red brick beauty cost a mere $9,999 to build. The square is lined with small businesses. The area has been referred to as "Cordell Hull Country" because the venerable former secretary of state under Franklin D. Roosevelt set up his first law practice in 1891 in Celina. Cordell Hull's former law office, an old cream-colored building, now a dentist's office, is on Dow Street, just off the square.

From 1933 until his retirement in 1944, Hull served as secretary of state. Author of the Good Neighbor Policy, the foundation of the current United Nations Organization, Hull was awarded the Nobel Peace Prize in 1945.

The Clay County Museum and Clay County Chamber of Commerce are housed in a log cabin on Brown Street. It's easy to find—just look for a big steam engine parked out front. Enclosed in glass, the steam engine is a symbol of Clay County's history. When the nearby 27,000-acre Dale Hollow Lake was created in 1943 by the U.S. Army Corps of Engineers, it buried houses, farms, buildings, cars, trees—you name it. A whole community was underwater, including the mammoth steam engine. Originally used for threshing grain, the steam engine was manufactured in 1906. Some divers found it in 1986 and the Corps of Engineers lifted it out of sixty feet of water and refurbished it.

From Celina, take State 53 north to the Free Hills, Tennessee's only remaining all-black settlement and one of the last in the Southeast. Settled between 1830 and 1850, the 400-acre rocky area was named for Virginia Hill, a white woman originally from North Carolina, who gave the original black settlers the land.

Hill brought four of the original settlers to the area when they were children. To this day, no one knows whether the children were slaves she had freed or if they were her biracial children she brought to the hills to keep safe. Named Ruben, Josh, Betty, and Maria Hill, the first four residents of the area later married. Betty is said to have married Bye Stone, a freed slave who took her surname.

By 1850, there were five black households; by 1860, there were eight black households—all with the surname Hill. The community continued to grow and flourish, and by the 1950s there were 400 residents, several dance halls, restaurants, grocery stores, and churches. Today, there are only sixty to seventy residents, and the population is steadily decreasing, says Clorina Andrews, who has run the Hilltop Cafe in Free Hills for twenty-nine years with her husband, George Andrews. "A lot of the young ones have moved away," Clorina explains. "They leave for jobs and go to school. Hopefully, some of them will eventually come back."

The Andrewses live next door to their restaurant, famous for Clorina's brown sugar pie and fried catfish. The small, comfortable restaurant with plastic tablecloths and ceiling fans has the feel of a family home. Although the Andrewses have no children, pictures of neighborhood children hang on the walls beside a photo of Dr. Martin Luther King, Jr., and a mirror adorned with pink flamingos. The café serves southern-style meat and vegetable buffets during the week and a short-order grill on Saturday. It's closed Sunday and Monday.

The Andrewses know most of their customers by name. If you're a stranger, Clorina will be glad to sit down, share a glass of iced tea, and talk about the history of the hills. That is, if she's not too busy. "I guess something between fifty and seventy people come through here a day," says Clorina, her brown eyes shining. "A lot of people just buy the pies and cakes. I have six caramel pies to make Friday for a wedding supper."

Back on State 53, go north to the entrance of the Dale Hollow Dam and the Dale Hollow National Fish Hatchery. Operated by the U.S. Fish and Wildlife Service, it is one of only two national fish hatcheries in the state. Nestled on thirty acres, the operation includes the hatchery, raceways of trout, and an aquarium filled with redear sunfish, large-mouth bass, bluegill, smallmouth bass, and spotted bass.

The hatchery receives about three million rainbow and brown trout eggs annually from locations all over the country. The eggs are then kept in incubator trays with forty-eight-degree water running over them constantly until they hatch. Then the baby fish are moved to long, rectangular blue concrete tanks filled with constantly flowing cold water. Fed high-protein fish food hourly, the trout grow an average of half an inch per month. When they're two to three inches long, the trout are transferred to outdoor raceways, where water flows through at approximately 8,000 gallons per minute. When the trout are eighteen months old, they're released into Kentucky and Tennessee lakes. The hatchery distributes more than 900,000 nine-inch rainbow trout annually.

Without cold-water hatcheries, we wouldn't have trout, explains Willis Smith, an animal keeper who works at the hatchery. "When we built dams, we did away with their natural habitats," Smith explains. "If they spawn in the river, when we generate electricity it washes away the eggs into the Cumberland River. They die because it's too warm there."

Most of the trout in the outdoor raceways are used for stocking once they reach nine inches, but the hatchery keeps some of the larger fish—one almost thirty-seven pounds—for viewing. Each raceway holds thousands of fish—not much personal space. The water rolls with brown and speckled trout, passing the time waiting to be fed.

One of the hatchery's highlights is watching the animal keeper feed the fish. When he approaches a raceway, the water starts to churn as the trout muscle their way past one another, swimming and jumping to catch the crumbs. But you don't have to be an animal keeper to get the trout going; they think every human being is a keeper with food. Just walk along a raceway and they'll swim with you like children following the pied piper.

Many of the homegrown trout are released in Dale Hollow Lake, arguably the prettiest lake in Tennessee. The lake was originally created when the U.S. Army Corps of Engineers built the Dale Hollow Dam for hydropower and flood control. Located in both Tennessee and Kentucky, Dale Hollow Lake is visited by more than four million people annually. The lake's clear blue waters are ideal for waterskiing, scuba diving, and fishing. The world record smallmouth bass, weighing in at eleven pounds fifteen ounces, was caught in this lake.

Back in Celina, take State 52 east to Livingston, the Overton County seat. Set in a picturesque valley, the town of 4,000 people has a charming square and a regal red brick courthouse that was built in 1868. Listed on the National Register of Historic Places, the Overton County Courthouse is surrounded by family-owned businesses and craft stores. One of the more interesting businesses blends country crafts with yesterday's treasures. The Court Square Emporium and Antique Mall, at 114 North Court Square, is filled with local crafts, antiques, vintage clothes and hats, antique jewelry, old photos, dishes, and quilts.

From Livingston, take State 85 out of town and look for State 42, a two-lane road to Cookeville. State 42 turns into a

Quilts, antiques, and crafts for sale

four-lane divided highway in Putnam County and becomes State 111/42 in Cookeville.

Cookeville, the Putnam County seat, has a stunning red brick courthouse off East Spring Street. Putnam County was organized in 1842 and named for Gen. Israel Putnam of the Revolutionary War. Soon after the county was established, however, an injunction restrained the county and circuit court officers from performing their duties because the county was supposedly improperly established. In 1854, the county was reestablished by Richard Cooke and the town was named for him.

The Tennessee Central Railroad came through here in 1890; the Cookeville Train Depot was built in 1909. Today, the original depot houses the Cookeville Depot Museum, a red brick building with windows trimmed in green, located at the corner of Cedar and Broad streets.

The building is unlike any Tennessee Central Train depot, explains Marilyn Brinker, director of the museum. "The floor plan is typical of Tennessee Central depots, but it's a brick building and that's unusual," she says. "And then it has a pagoda roofline, which makes it one of the most unusual Tennessee train depots. You normally see pagoda rooflines only in Asia. How we got the Oriental influence here at that time, no one knows."

Owned and maintained by Cookeville, the museum houses railroad memorabilia, railroad photographs, exhibits about the city's history, and Tennessee Central Railroad artifacts. There's also an L&N caboose out back. The L&N came through here after the Tennessee Central went bankrupt.

You can't miss the Cream City Ice Cream sign just across the street from the museum. Put up in 1950, the neon sign is twenty feet tall and thirty feet long, and the curvy letters practically jump off the building. When lit, the old-fashioned ice cream sign's individual letters blink on one at a time.

The sign made more sense back in 1950, when the building housed a local ice-cream producer. Today, the building and sign are owned by Bob and Myra Kernea, who screen print T-shirts for Cream City Tees. The Kerneas wouldn't think of taking down the sign. "If I did, I'd be run out of town," Bob Kernea says. "People love that sign. It's a Cookeville landmark."

If you're hungry for Italian food, Cookeville has just the eatery for you. Mamma Rosa's Italian Restaurant, at 1405 North Washington Avenue, serves pizza, pasta, and calzones, all made to order. Of course, you'd better like zesty tomato sauce and lots of mozzarella—it comes with everything.

Burgess Falls State Natural Area, located on the eastern edge of Tennessee's Highland Rim, is a charming spot in Cookeville. The area, off State 135 south, was named for Tom Burgess, who was deeded the land in 1793 by the government for his service in the Revolutionary War. There are hiking trails, scenic overlooks, and a 130-foot waterfall located in a large gorge on the Falling Water River. Pack a picnic, don your hiking boots, and enjoy some of nature's best.

In the Area

Armour's Red Boiling Springs Hotel (Red Boiling Springs): 615-699-2180

Burgess Falls State Natural Area (Cookeville): 615-432-5312

Clay County Chamber of Commerce (Celina): 615-243-3338

Cookeville Depot Museum (Cookeville): 615-528-8570

Court Square Emporium and Antique Mall (Livingston): 615-823-6741

Cream City Tees (Cookeville): 615-526-8222

Dale Hollow National Fish Hatchery (Celina): 615-243-2443

Donoho Hotel (Red Boiling Springs): 615-699-3141

Hilltop Cafe (Celina): 615-243-2698

Lafayette Key Park/Log House (Lafayette): 615-666-5885

Mamma Rosa's (Cookeville): 615-372-8694

Tennessee Technological University (Cookeville): 615-372-3101

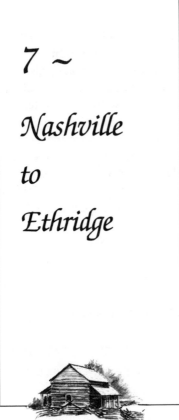

7 ~

Nashville

to

Ethridge

From Chattanooga, take I-24 west to Nashville. The total trip length from Nashville to Ethridge is 110 miles.

Highlights: *The opulence of Belmont Mansion, the musical history of the Ryman Auditorium, the art of Cheekwood, the live music of Bluebird Cafe, and the wonder of Athena Parthenos and the Parthenon—all in Nashville; the history of Carnton Plantation in Franklin; the home of James K. Polk in Columbia; the simplicity of the Green Valley General Store in Bodenham; and the Amish community in Ethridge.*

From the musicmakers to the acres of unsullied parks to the stunning architecture to the history of a town that began as a salt lick, Nashville is one phenomenal place.

Of course, I'm a little biased. My husband and I grew up in Nashville, the capital of Tennessee since 1843. It's a city that's friendly to strangers and comfortable with stars—the kind of place where *everyone,* including your hairdresser, is a songwriter or singer; where you're likely to see country performer Emmylou Harris buying groceries at Kroger or guitar great Phil Keaggy performing at church while ushers take up the offering.

Nashville's a big town with small-town charm. It's big enough to have an international airport and small enough that people often give directions around town using churches as landmarks. Since we have 800 churches, it can get pretty confusing.

Back before the churches and commerce, Nashville served as a hunting ground for the prehistoric Indians in 8000 B.C. The last Indians to live here were the Shawnees in the eighteenth century. The first white men to come through Nashville were French traders; one of them set up a trading post on salty Lick Branch near the Cumberland River, just north of Nashville's downtown business district. Daniel Boone and Kasper Mansker came to scout out the area in 1770. By 1780, more than 300 settlers had come for good. James Robertson led a group of people by land from North Carolina to French Lick, then a part of North Carolina. John Donelson led a second group in a flotilla of thirty-three boats down the Holston River, up the Ohio River, and up the Cumberland River. The area was named Nashborough, after General Francis Nash of North Carolina.

In 1796, Tennessee became the sixteenth state; Nashville was named the permanent capital in 1843. The Tennessee State Capitol, near the intersection of Seventh Avenue North and Charlotte Avenue, was built between 1845 and 1859. Designed by William Strickland, the limestone building features massive columns and extensive cast iron. It remains one of the most highly regarded Greek Revival–style buildings in the nation.

The capitol's lawn is adorned with statues of Sam Davis, "Boy Hero of the Confederacy"; Alvin C. York, World War I hero; and the (Andrew) Jackson Equestrian Statue, of which there are two others in Washington, D.C., and New Orleans. Notice the six cedar trees on the lawn: they were planted in the mid-1980s to commemorate the six million Jews who died as a result of the Holocaust.

Ryman Auditorium, home of the Grand Ole Opry, 1943–1974

An example of Egyptian Revival architecture, the Downtown Presbyterian Church, at 154 Fifth Avenue North, was also designed by Strickland. Egyptian columns rise on either side of the front of the building; the sanctuary resembles the temple to the sun god Amon Ra, in Karnak, Egypt. Designed to create the feeling of walking into an Egyptian temple, the sanctuary includes appropriate wall paintings, woodwork, and stained glass windows. Winged sun discs, a symbol of the sun god, can be seen above the entrances to the church and also above the altar.

The Ryman Auditorium, a Victorian Gothic–style building on Fifth Avenue North, was the home of the Grand Ole Opry from 1943 to 1974. Built in the 1890s by Thomas G. Ryman, a wealthy steamboat captain, the building was originally the Union Gospel Tabernacle, an all-faith meeting hall. Ryman built the huge, 3,000-seat building after Rev. Sam Jones brought Ryman to Christ.

Upon the captain's death in 1904, the building was renamed the Ryman. Because of its acoustics and seating capacity, the building eventually became the unofficial city auditorium, hosting religious services, meetings, rallies, political conventions, and plenty of stars, such as Will Rogers, Orson Welles, and Katharine Hepburn. Visitors can see the dressing rooms and stand on the stage where musical greats such as Marian Anderson and Elvis Presley once performed. During the thirty-one years the Grand Ole Opry called the Ryman home, the sold-out weekend shows featured folks such as Patsy Cline, Willie Nelson, Ernest Tubb, Marty Robbins, and Jim Reeves.

Many of those early entertainers would have come to town by an L&N train and arrived at the Union Station, at 1001 Broadway. Built in 1900, the station is one of Nashville's most loved landmarks. The Richardsonian Romanesque Revival–style multi-story building, with its elegant clock tower, was built by the L&N Railroad; it now houses a hotel and restaurants. While you're there, look behind the station at the huge shed, with an iron truss system spanning more than 200 feet. It's also a favorite spot for pigeons, so be careful.

The Second Avenue Historic District is Nashville's oldest area. Built between the 1870s and 1890s, the buildings are an impressive collection of Victorian façades. Most of the antique, block-deep former warehouses also front on First Avenue and the Cumberland River, speaking to Nashville's history as a river port. Some of the buildings' façades have been altered in the twentieth century to include more windows and cleaner, simpler lines. As you walk along the street, notice the dates of construction on the buildings, which today house restaurants, trendy shops, residences, and nightclubs. Parking along this one-way street can be challenging, but there are parking garages on Commerce Street and Second Avenue North.

One of the city's most unique architectural offerings is the Parthenon, in Centennial Park on the corner of West End and Centennial avenues. This full-scale replica of the Parthenon in Athens, Greece, is a one-of-a-kind copy, with columns, sculptures of gods and goddesses in the pediments—the whole works. It's open Tuesday through Saturday.

Built in 1897 of brick, wooden lath, and plaster, the Parthenon was the centerpiece of a Centennial Exposition celebrating Tennessee's first hundred years of statehood. The enormous structure reflected the city's reputation as the "Athens of the South." When the temporary structure began falling down, the Park Board decided to rebuild it with permanent materials. Since its reopening in 1931, the Parthenon has remained virtually unchanged, except for a twenty-month renovation in 1987.

Inside, there's a visitors center and gift shop and a nicely laid out museum featuring rotating exhibits in the East and West galleries. The permanent collection in the Cowan Gallery includes works by artists Winslow Homer and William Merritt Chase. On the second floor, you'll find a replica of Athena

Parthenos in all her glory. Turn the corner of the stairs and look *up*. The forty-two-foot-tall goddess took Nashville sculptor Alan LeQuire and friends almost eight years to create. Made of gypsum cement and chopped fiberglass, Athena has a commanding presence, to say the least. Standing on a five-foot-tall marble pedestal, the goddess supports a seventeen-foot shield with her left hand; in her outstretched right hand is Nike, the winged goddess of victory, holding a golden wreath to place on Athena's head.

Phidias created the original Athena for the Parthenon in Athens in the fifth century B.C. LeQuire's copy of Athena is the largest piece of indoor sculpture in the Western world. To support her massive weight, a steel beam extends from her shoulders, through her body, through the second and first floors of the building, and into the ground.

Known as the goddess of warfare and the arts, among other things, Athena faces the west entrance of the Parthenon and its two tall doors, which are usually open. The bronze doors are the largest in the world—each leaf weighs 7.5 tons. Walk through the doorway to an open area for a good view of the west pediment, which portrays Athena fighting with Poseidon for control of the land of Attica. The east pediment shows Athena at her birth, surrounded by gods and goddesses.

Centennial Park, home of the Parthenon, gets its name from the Centennial Exposition. Surrounded by commerce and fronted by busy West End Avenue, the park is a wide, open place to throw a Frisbee, fly a kite, or have a picnic. There's a playground, two-person swings, flat roads perfect for roller blading, and Watauga Lake—a great place to feed the ducks.

The Metropolitan Historical Commission offers guided walking tours of Nashville that include the buildings listed above and others, including the Broadway Historic District; Printers Alley; the Arcade, a 1903 structure inspired by a mall in Milan, Italy; and the Hermitage Hotel, a 1920s Beaux

Arts–style hotel. The commission also offers brochures for a Civil War driving tour and an African-American history tour. For more information on the tours, call the commission at 615-862-7970.

If touring downtown makes you hungry, there are two Nashville traditions nearby. Swett's Restaurant, at 2725 Clifton Avenue, is a country food lover's dream. Swett's has been in business since 1954, although the original building burned to the ground in 1988. The current restaurant has the same great food—fried chicken, chicken-fried steak, turnip greens, mashed potatoes, pinto beans, creamed corn, and cherry cobbler. Swett's plates also come with corn bread, butter, and onion slices.

If you want something a little different, try the Gerst Haus, a rambunctious German eatery at 228 Woodland Street. Wooden tables with red-and-white checkered tablecloths fill a large dining area whose walls are lined with Nashville memorabilia. The restaurant serves all kinds of sandwiches, salads, bratwurst sausage, pig knuckles, and corned beef and cabbage. Their specialty is Gerst beer—big steins of it. Brewed from 1890 to 1955 at the Gerst Brewery in Nashville, the beer is now produced in Evansville, Indiana. Try the ham rolls, oyster rolls, and Gerst beer. The food's good, the beer's plentiful, and the fun factor is high. You can dance to an oompah band playing German music on Saturday and Sunday nights.

For a taste of Nashville's history, take a tour of Travellers Rest, at 636 Farrell Parkway. Home of Judge John Overton from 1799 to 1833, it is the oldest house in Nashville open to the public. The Federal-style house was built on a 960-acre plantation known for its fine cotton and peaches.

As a young lawyer, Overton migrated to Tennessee from Virginia and made his fortune settling land claims along the western frontier. Serving as Tennessee Supreme Court judge, Overton wrote many of the state's land laws. He also founded the city of Memphis.

Today, the two-story white clapboard home with green shutters lies on eleven of the original 960 acres. Decorated to represent 1799, the earliest part of Overton's life here, many of the rooms still have the feel of a bachelor's pad—especially a main room downstairs with painted dark green walls, sparse decorations, and solid furniture. Travellers Rest has the state's largest collection of pre-1840 Tennessee-made furniture.

Overton was the law partner, confidante, and campaign manager of Andrew Jackson, the seventh president of the United States. The men remained close friends until Overton's death in 1833. Yet there's one real mystery about the man. "He was very fastidious and kept records of everything," says Angelia Hartline, director of communications and programs for Travellers Rest. "And we have some of those. But at the time of his death, he had every paper related to Andrew Jackson burned. They had so many business dealings—nobody knows what was in those papers."

Travellers Rest hosts many events throughout the year, including the annual Twelfth Night Celebration, a festival of eating, drinking, and merrymaking held around Christmas. Hostesses in period costumes give candlelight tours of the house, which is decorated with fruit and greenery.

One of Nashville's fine homes that's often overlooked is Belmont Mansion, on the campus of Belmont University, at 1900 Belmont Boulevard. Built in 1850 by Joseph and Adelicia Acklen, it is the fifth largest house in Nashville, with thirty-six rooms and almost 20,000 square feet of living space.

As you walk through the Italian villa with marble statues and the original gasoliers and mirrors, you can almost hear the nasal British accent of Robin Leach, of "Lifestyles of the Rich and Famous": Feast your eyes, if you will, upon the genuine marble sculpture by William H. Rinehart. . . .

Adelicia, a beautiful socialite whose biography was published in an antique tome, *Queens of American Society*, held glittering balls and flawless receptions at the summer home.

"Adelicia is thought to have been the basis of Margaret Mitchell's character Scarlet O'Hara in *Gone With the Wind*," says John Lancaster, interpreter.

A tour of fifteen of the mansion's rooms includes both period and original furniture and art. Adelicia was an avid art collector, owning more than 200 pieces of original art—the largest personal collection in the South in the 1860s.

Adelicia literally shopped "til she dropped." At the age of seventy, she died of pneumonia in a Fifth Avenue Hotel while on a shopping spree in New York City. Upon her death, the mansion became a college—named the Belmont College for Young Women. Three more buildings were added on in 1890, including the white Colonial mansion that faces Wedgewood Avenue—the building most people think of as Belmont Mansion. In 1913, the school became Ward Belmont, a fashionable women's school and Grand Ole Opry entertainer Minnie Pearl's alma mater. The mansion was reopened to the public in 1976.

Throughout the year, the mansion offers events and classical concerts by the delightful Belmont Camerata Musicale. The best time to visit is during the summer, when school isn't in session and parking places are plentiful. If you visit during the school year, Saturday is the best day for parking.

Another notable period house worth visiting in Nashville is Cheekwood, at 1200 Forrest Park Drive. The eighteenth-century English manor features outstanding European architectural details as well as acclaimed art. Constructed in 1932 during the Depression, the mansion was owned by Mr. and Mrs. Leslie Cheek, heirs to the Maxwell House coffee fortune. The Cheeks traveled in Europe with their architect, Bryant Fleming, searching for the right details for their home: a marble mantelpiece from an English home, a pair of intricately carved mahogany fruitwood doors from the home of the Duke of Westminster, a delicate crystal chandelier from Austria. From the Palladian window and the English mantelpiece carved with figures of the Parade of Bacchus in the drawing room to the incredible Adamesque mantel of lapis lazuli in an upstairs dining room, every detail is exquisite.

Today, the mansion houses a permanent collection of American art from the nineteenth and twentieth centuries, Worchester porcelains, antique silver, Oriental snuff bottles, and period furniture. One of the most interesting exhibits features work by visionary artist William Edmondson, a Nashville-born laborer, fireman, janitor, and stonecutter. At some point in his life, "God told Edmondson" to carve figures out of limestone. His crude Biblical figures include small animals, preachers, nurses, hospital patients, and everyday people—all portrayed with humor and insight. Discovered in the 1930s, Edmondson became the first African-American to have a one-person exhibit in the Museum of Modern Art in New York City.

Cheekwood's luxuriant lawns and beautifully manicured gardens make for a peaceful walk in the park. During the summer, Cheekwood hosts jazz and classical concerts on the lawn.

Millions of people annually visit Percy and Edwin Warner Park, 2,264 acres of rolling hills, winding roads, and hiking trails, off State 100 just past Old Hickory Boulevard. Tree covered and rustic, the park is a great getaway whether you like to walk, ride a bike, picnic, ride a horse, throw a Frisbee, or just watch the stars. Far from the city lights, the park is a favorite spot for watching meteor showers and the Fourth of July fireworks.

The park also hosts the annual Iroquois Steeplechase, the richest amateur steeplechase in the United States, with a purse of some $155,000. Held in May, the event is attended by more than 50,000 people. It's a good time on the lawn for folks with folding chairs, picnics, and beer. For those inside the gates, it's a social affair of hats and gloves and pleasant smiles. If you attend the event, wear something comfortable and bring suntan lotion, a blanket or a beach towel, and binoculars. Be forewarned: glass containers aren't allowed.

A few miles west of the park, at 8500 State 100, is the Loveless Motel and Restaurant, a rural café that serves fried chicken, primo country ham, redeye gravy, homemade preserves, and fluffy biscuits. The decor includes an old-time cash register that rings seventy cents permanently, wooden floors, and simple tables. Opened in the 1950s, the home-style eatery has an enclosed front porch where people wait to be seated. The walls are lined with old signed photographs of country stars, including Chet Atkins and Charlie Pride, and pictures of "Hee Haw" performers.

Catering to all walks of life, the country eating establishment stays pretty busy. If you're visiting for dinner or on a weekend, reservations are suggested. When we were there for breakfast, the gravel parking lot was filled with everything from BMWs to pickup trucks to Harley Davidson motorcycles.

Thousands of people come to Nashville each year just for the music. Any night of the week, you can hear live bluegrass at nightclubs, such as Douglas Corner Cafe, at 2106-A 8th Avenue South, or at Station Inn, at 402 12th Avenue South.

Our favorite club is the Bluebird Cafe, at 4104 Hillsboro Pike, a popular haunt for some of the hottest songwriters and singers around. The small, dimly lit club has wooden tables and chairs and seats along the bar. Reservations are suggested for Friday and Saturday nights, when the club is generally standing room only. If it's a writers-in-the-round night, usually four songwriters will sit in a circle, facing each other, and take turns singing their own songs. They also play along with each other and sing harmony if they know the melody.

Often the songs are old hits that take on a new character with the songwriter's voice. Or they're new tunes that haven't made it onto an album. Some of the songs may never be more than scraps of paper with scribbled lyrics. But when the writer strums his guitar and sings a song that he may even change on the way home, it's like Michelangelo stopping in the middle of painting the Sistine Chapel and asking a passerby, Hey, how does that look?

If you want to see where plenty of hitmakers have cut some of the world's most-loved songs, take a tour of RCA Studio B, part of the Country Music Hall of Fame, at Four Music Square East. Opened in 1957, RCA's original studio was the site of some big recordings, including songs by Dolly Parton, Chet Atkins, and the Everly Brothers. The most famous person to lift his voice in this room, however, was Elvis Presley, who made more than 200 recordings at Studio B before it closed in 1977.

A forty-minute tour of the studio includes a view of Nipper the dog, RCA's trademark since 1929; an audio history of the studio, narrated by Dolly Parton, Chet Atkins, and Waylon Jennings, in the studio; and an audio presentation about the songs that were recorded in the control room. Although there are plenty of real-live, state-of-the-art recording studios in Nashville, they're not open for viewing by the general public. Studio B gives visitors a first-person look at a mixing board and original instruments that would have been used during those famous recordings.

Other offerings in the Nashville area include: the Cumberland Science Museum (800 Ridley Boulevard), a hands-on children's museum offering exhibits on everything from dinosaurs to space; the Belle Meade Plantation (5025 Harding Road), an 1853 Greek Revival mansion that served as the centerpiece of a 5,300-acre plantation and thoroughbred farm; the Van Vechten Gallery (1000 17th Avenue North), on the campus of Fisk University, housing a collection of more than a hundred pieces, including works by Cézanne, Renoir, and O'Keeffe; Opryland (2802 Opryland Drive), a theme park known for its rides and excellent live music shows; the Grand Ole Opry (2804 Opryland Drive), home of the live radio broadcast featuring country music's old and new performers;

The Hermitage (4580 Rachel's Lane, Hermitage), the stately two-story home of Andrew Jackson, the seventh president of the United States; the Oscar L. Farris Agricultural Museum, located at the Ellington Agricultural Center (corner of Hogan Road and Marchant Avenue), which pays homage to Tennessee's rich agricultural history; and Radnor Lake State Natural Area (1160 Otter Creek Road), offering well-worn hiking trails around a shimmering lake.

If you love old cemeteries, Mt. Olivet Cemetery, at 1101 Lebanon Road, is a must-walk-through. Established in 1856, the 250-acre cemetery has been a final resting place for an estimated 190,000 people, including Judge John Overton, Adelicia Acklen, and Thomas G. Ryman. Carvings on the sides of the Ryman monument show his livelihood: there's a steamboat on one side and a fishing skiff on the other. Adelicia Acklen's Gothic family mausoleum features bronze doors and a marble statue of Peri inside.

From Nashville, take US 431 south to Franklin, a charming town named for Benjamin Franklin. Founded in 1799, the town was a bustle of activity by the 1800s, with lawyers, doctors, ministers, gunsmiths, and wagonmakers moving in.

Franklin is still growing. The Williamson County seat brims with small-town charm, and its downtown square is arguably the prettiest in all of Tennessee. Wonderfully laid out, the square features a monument of a Confederate soldier; Victorian and modern buildings rim the square.

The entire fifteen-block original downtown area, including the Main Street shopping district, is listed on the National Register of Historic Places. Walk around and visit the boutiques, art galleries, gift shops, and antique stores, all housed in restored nineteenth-century buildings.

Some of Franklin's historic downtown buildings include the McPhail Office, built on Main Street before 1839 and used by Dr. Daniel McPhail for his medical practice, where he reportedly administered the first anesthetic used successfully in central Tennessee; the Williamson County Courthouse, a white-columned, red brick building on Third Avenue South, constructed in 1859; and St. Paul's Episcopal Church, on Fifth Avenue North. Built in 1831, the church was used during the Civil War as a hospital; its pews, pulpit, and furnishings were burned as firewood and its organ pipes were strewn up and down the streets of Franklin. The only items that escaped destruction were the church records and altar silver, which were buried across the street during the church's occupation.

Many of Franklin's historic buildings, including Carnton Plantation and the Carter House, suffered damage during the Battle of Franklin. Although the bloody battle lasted only five hours on November 30, 1864, the skirmish saw some 8,578 Americans killed, wounded, or taken prisoner.

Carnton Plantation, at 1345 Carnton Lane, was used as a hospital during the fierce battle. A doctor operated in the parlor and the porch became a temporary morgue. Six Confederate generals lost their lives in the battle, four of whom were laid out on the porch—Generals Cleburne, Granbury, Strahl, and Adams.

The plantation was named after Carn town, a township in Ireland where the owner of the house was born. Ironically enough, the township's name meant "marking a memorable event." The name certainly held true in 1864. There are permanent bloodstains near the fireplace and window in the upstairs bedroom and on the back porch from the more than 200 Confederate soldiers who were taken in on the day of the battle.

The interior of the huge home is simple, with wide open rooms and period furniture. Family portraits of John and Caroline McGavock, the original owners, are hung in the downstairs parlor.

In 1866, John McGavock decided to bring the remains of 1,481 soldiers from their temporary graves to Carnton for permanent burial near a grove of trees in the front of the lot.

The McGavock Cemetery is the largest private Confederate cemetery in the country.

The mansion is rumored to be haunted. "People have seen General Cleburne's ghost sitting on the back porch," says a docent for the mansion. "He usually gets up and walks inside the house."

Also in the area is the Carter House, at 1140 Columbia Avenue. The home was caught in the cross fire during the Civil War. Built in 1830 by Fountain Branch Carter, the registered National Historic Landmark was used as a Federal post during the Battle of Franklin. The family, neighbors, and servants hid in the cellar for five hours while the fighting raged overhead. A tour includes the museum, a battlerama video, and a look at the house, whose façade was punctured with bullets and whose door was broken open by a Union soldier, looking for refuge during the battle.

From Franklin, take US 31 south through Spring Hill. The road passes beautiful antebellum homes and farms. Nestled on some 2,400 acres is General Motors' Saturn plant, the only place in America where the car is made. Hidden by low hills, the massive car manufacturing facility blends into the surrounding small town because it looks like a horse farm with miles of white fences.

Columbia is about twelve miles farther south on US 31. The Maury County seat, Columbia is the former home of our nation's eleventh president. The James K. Polk Home, a registered National Historic Landmark, was built in 1816. A tour of the estate, located on West 7th Street, includes the main house, kitchen, and the Sisters' House next door, where Polk's sisters once lived. Many of the furnishings in the home were used by the Polks in the White House. Highlights of the tour include the inaugural Bible used by Polk, pieces of four services of china from the White House, Mrs. Polk's Parisian ball gown, and a fan Polk had made for Mrs. Polk to carry to the inaugural ball.

Historians refer to Polk as one of our greatest presidents, because he took office with four campaign goals and left office having completed them all. They included settling the Oregon question; reducing the tariff; reestablishing an independent treasury; and purchasing California, making it the first time the United States stretched from the Atlantic to the Pacific ocean.

Besides being Polk's stomping grounds, Columbia is known as the "Mule Trading Capital of America." Columbia became a center for mule (a hybrid offspring of a jack and a mare) trading in 1840s. Young mules were shipped in from Missouri and sold or traded to sugar plantations in the South. The street sales became nationally known, and by 1934 the city decided to turn it into a celebration called "Market Day." Except for a break during war years, it's been a tradition ever since. Held annually in April, the event includes mule shows, mule auctions, mule pulling contests, and the hilarious "Wild Mule Race." There's also a Saturday night square dance and a major knife show.

From Columbia, take US 43 west through Mount Pleasant, and then State 166 south to US 64 east to Pulaski, the Giles County seat. Giles County and Pulaski were established in 1809. In 1887, a raging fire destroyed the courthouse and all of the businesses and homes around the square, prompting the city fathers to pass an ordinance that all future buildings be made from either brick or stone.

Today, the Pulaski business district is on the National Register of Historic Places. The Giles County Courthouse, built in 1909, is one of the finest in central Tennessee. The Neoclassical building with tall Corinthian columns stands proud and tall in the center of town.

For some great eating, check out LawLers Barbecue on US 64—a drive-through barbecue place housed in a plain brown brick building. Orders are placed through a sliding glass

Two participants in Columbia's Market Day

window on the side of the structure. They serve spicy ribs, barbecue sandwiches, tangy coleslaw, baked beans, and rolls.

Pulaski has several historic districts, one of which is the Sam Davis Avenue Historic District. Beautiful Tudor and Victorian homes along Sam Davis Avenue represent architecture from 1860 to 1910. A sign in front of each home indicates the name of the owner and the year the house was built. Walk or ride along this shady street to get a feel for yesterday.

The area was named for Sam Davis, "Boy Hero of the Confederacy." During the Civil War, Davis was captured by the Union army; he refused to divulge any information to the enemy and was hanged as a spy by Union soldiers. A statue stands on the south side of the public square to commemorate Davis's bravery. The Sam Davis Museum is located on Sam Davis Avenue, but to see the interior of the building, you have to call the manager at 615-363-3888.

Nearby is the Old Graveyard Memorial Park, on the corner of US 31 and Cemetery Street. Used from 1817 to 1833, the cemetery has been refurbished and the markers have been repaired. Ranging from plain and simple to ornate, the more than 200 monuments list births as early as 1753.

From Pulaski, take US 64 west and look for a sign for the Green Valley General Store. Housed in a dark brown wooden building, the store's entire front façade is hidden behind farm tools and implements. Owned by Morris and Becky Williams, the store is a treasure of quilts and Amish crafts, with a delicatessen selling home-baked sweets and bread, fresh lemonade, and fried apple and peach pies. Cured hams and antique farm gear hang from the ceiling of the store.

The Williamses, who make their home in the top story of the store, opened their business as a big peach and apple shed in 1986. "It was just going to be a big fruit store because we had our peach and apple orchards across the road," says

Becky Williams. "Then we added a couple of cookies and then a couple of brownies and it just grew and grew. The secret of our success is simplicity and wholesomeness. I try to keep things good and simple."

Lawrenceburg, the next stop along US 64, is the Lawrence County seat. The first permanent settlements in the county were established along Big Buffalo River, still a wild river today. One of Tennessee's most famous native sons, Davy Crockett, moved to Lawrence County in 1817. The pioneer and soldier helped establish the county after the land was ceded by the Chickasaw Indians to the United States. Crockett also served as a justice of the peace, a colonel of the militia, and a state representative.

A large bronze statue of Crockett stands in the middle of the town square, which is lined with small shops and antique stores. The David Crockett State Park, located just west of Lawrenceburg on US 64, was established in 1959 and has recreational and camping facilities, a swimming pool, and a restaurant.

David Crockett's Office and Museum lie south of the square on South Military Avenue. A replica of Crockett's log cabin office contains a bag used to carry shooting gear, a wooden canteen, a broadax, clothes, writings, and other Crockett memorabilia, all in glass cases. The unattended cabin stays open from 8:00 A.M. to sundown. There's no lock on the door—even though it feels like you're trespassing.

From Lawrenceburg, take US 43 north past open farmland to Ethridge, a small town that wasn't incorporated until 1973. It began as a railroad stop in 1883. Today, Ethridge is known for its large community of more than 200 Amish families. The religious group moved here in 1944 because of the rich, flat farmland. The Amish doctrine requires farming and personal simplicity as a way of life. Men wear beards and wide-brimmed hats, and women wear long, dark dresses.

The Amish conduct church services and school in their homes. They don't believe in using modern "evils" such as electricity. For the most part, they don't drive cars, but use horse-pulled buggies for transportation. They make their money from farming and the sale of handcrafted items.

You'll find some of these items, such as the quilts and pottery, at the Amish Country Galleries, located in a renovated motel at 3931 US 43 north. Owned by Dave Williams, the four-year-old store also features handcrafted rocking chairs and other wooden furniture. Working with Amish families over the years has taught Williams to live with their lifestyle. Some people, however, still mind driving slowly behind horse-drawn buggies. "I wouldn't say it interferes with traffic," he comments. "But it irritates some people because they have to slow down."

To drive through the Amish community, turn left onto a dirt road past the crafts mall. You'll see neatly kept houses and barns, tilled land, Belgian draft horses, and small bales of oats and wheat in the fields. Children in dark clothes and straw hats can be seen playing in the yard as their mother sweeps the porch.

Most Amish don't like to have their pictures taken, says Williams. And they don't usually take kindly to strangers' questions. Many of them, however, advertise fresh vegetables, sorghum molasses, or homemade candy for sale on signs in their front yards. Feel free to visit and buy. If they offer peanut brittle, buy it—it's as good as my grandmother's.

In the Area

Amish Country Galleries (Ethridge): 615-829-2126

Belle Meade Plantation (Nashville): 615-356-0501

Belmont Mansion (Nashville): 615-269-9537

Bluebird Cafe (Nashville): 615-383-1461

Carnton Plantation (Franklin): 615-794-0903

Carter House (Franklin): 615-791-1861

Cheekwood, Tennessee Botanical Gardens and Museum of Art (Nashville): 615-353-2163

Country Music Hall of Fame (Nashville): 615-256-1639

David Crockett State Park (Lawrenceburg): 615-762-9408

Cumberland Science Museum (Nashville): 615-862-5160

Oscar L. Farris Agricultural Museum (Nashville): 615-360-0197

Grand Ole Opry (Nashville): 615-889-3060

Green Valley General Store (Bodenham): 615-363-6562

The Hermitage (Hermitage): 615-889-2941

LawLers Barbecue (Pulaski): 615-363-3515

Loveless Motel and Restaurant (Nashville): 615-646-9700

The Metropolitan Historical Commission (Nashville): 615-862-7970

Mt. Olivet Cemetery (Nashville): 615-255-4193

Opryland (Nashville): 615-889-6611

Parthenon (Nashville): 615-862-8431

James K. Polk Home (Columbia): 615-388-2354

Radnor Lake State Natural Area (Nashville): 615-377-1281

Ryman Auditorium (Nashville): 615-254-1445

Swett's Restaurant (Nashville): 615-329-4418

Tennessee State Capitol (Nashville): 615-741-2692

Tours (Nashville): 615-244-7835

Travellers Rest (Nashville): 615-832-2962

Van Vechten Gallery (Nashville): 615-329-8543

Warner Park Nature Center (Nashville): 615-352-6299

8 ~

Adams

to

Dover

From **Nashville,** take I-24 west to Coopertown, then take County 256 north about ten miles to Adams. The total trip length from Adams to Dover is about ninety miles.

Highlights: *The Bell Witch of Adams; the Port Royal covered bridge; Plummer's Old Store Orchard and Museum; the Clarksville Montgomery County Museum, one of the best small museums in the state; and Beachaven Vineyards and Winery, with a picnic area to share your purchases.*

Adams is a beautiful little farming town of friendly people, fields of tobacco and corn, and a creek for canoeing. It's not the kind of place you'd expect to find a legendary witch.

My sisters and I grew up with a healthy fear of Adams's Bell Witch, the vicious spirit that began haunting the Bell family in 1818. The mere mention of her name would send us all flying under the covers. We grew up believing that if you stood in a dark room in front of a mirror, turned around three times, and then said "Bell Witch," she'd appear. To this day, I don't know if it works—I was never brave enough to try it.

115

The Bell Witch is perhaps the most documented story of the supernatural. The following information was taken from M. V. Ingram's *An Authenticated History of the Famous Bell Witch of Tennessee*, a book based on eyewitness accounts and interviews, which was published in 1894.

It all began with scratching noises and tapping sounds at the front door—noises John Bell attributed to pranksters. Soon after that, three Bell sons were awakened by a noise that sounded like a rat gnawing on the bedpost—a noise that stopped when the lights were lit and continued when it was dark. The noise became a nightly occurrence, traveling from room to room until everyone was awake. New sounds were added—a large dog chewing on the door, chairs falling over, chains dragging, and gulping sounds as if someone were choking. And bedcovers were being pulled off the beds.

Then the Bell Witch got serious. She started pulling hair until the Bell children were writhing in pain. Pretty soon, everyone knew about the haunting, and various people came to offer advice, including Gen. Andrew Jackson. As Jackson's party of men approached the house, Jackson's wagon wheels suddenly locked. That night, the witch boxed one of the men on his nose and sent him running home.

Eventually the witch began talking to the Bell family and their visitors. The spirit said in a disembodied feminine voice that she was the "Old Kate Batts Witch." Batts was a neighbor of Bell's—a woman with whom he had a falling-out before she died. The witch pledged to kill Bell before it was all over. True to her word, the Bell Witch poisoned him and then showed up at his funeral singing drunkenly.

Bell Witch sightings or hearings have been reported throughout the years. The witch supposedly now lives in a cave, and people in the area love talking about their famous spirit.

Nina Seely named her store in honor of old Kate. The Bell Witch Village Antique Mall is located off US 41 in Adams, in the old abandoned Bell High School. "I came back here to save the old school," says Seely. "Now people come from all over to hear about the Bell Witch."

Seely, an antique dealer and licensed appraiser, runs the business with the help of her husband, Roy Pryor. The store has five rooms full of antiques, furniture, old records, knick-knacks, and dishes from about ten dealers. One whole hall-way is covered with photographs, many of them signed, of would-be country music stars.

Seely and Pryor are also singers, performing in the Bell Witch Opry every Saturday night. With the help of the Bell Witch Opry staff band, the couple puts on a show of country and pop songs in the school's old gymnasium: visitors sit in the school's original foldout wooden seats and the band performs on the old high school stage.

"We try to promote older and younger people in country music," says Seely. "Dolly Parton came here one time. And Buddy Spicher [of Grand Ole Opry fame] still plays here every once in a while."

Pryor, seventy, sings the pop music and Seely sings the country. She says, "I never get on the show when I don't have to sing 'Satin Sheets.' "

Pryor met Seely when he came to tune the old piano upstairs in the gymnasium. He jokes, "Nina likes antiques so much she married one."

Visitors ask the local couple questions about the Bell Witch. Pryor says he hasn't seen her, even though their store is located only a few miles from the witch's cave. Seely, on the other hand, swears she hears "strange" noises all the time. "I hear things—unusual voices and things," Seely says. "One day when I was upstairs, I heard a lot of moving noises. I got so scared, I practically rode down the railing of the stairs."

A mile or so east on US 41 from the Bell Witch Village Antique Mall is the Bellwood Cemetery. Established in the 1960s by descendants of the Bell family, the cemetery is surrounded by a two-foot-high concrete wall. A twenty-foot obelisk with a ball on top stands at the upper end of the plot. The inscription reads, "To the Glory of God." Family members' names are engraved on the monument as well.

From Adams, take State 76 west to County 238 and go north over Sulpher Fork Creek, a meandering stretch of water. The two-lane blacktop road winds through farmland and green grassy fields on the way to the Port Royal State Historic Area.

When you come to the W. D. Pete Hudson bridge, you'll be right across from the romantic Port Royal covered bridge, a barn-lumber structure spanning the Red River. Walking through the bridge, you can hear the water running below and see the shafts of light play upon the rafters. Besides the bridge, there are also some great picnic spots along the scenic river. This is a perfect family kind of place, or just a beautiful stop to stretch your legs.

Back on State 76, go west until you see Plummer's Old Store Orchard and Museum, just a few miles east of Clarksville. H. B. and Mildred Plummer's little-bit-of-everything store is easy to miss because it doesn't look open. But it's open most days, unless the Plummers are out fishing.

The Plummers opened the store thirty-five years ago. They have five children, six grandchildren, and 455 tomato plants—that is, if you're visiting in the summer. Genuinely good people, the Montgomery County natives both grew up here and like the "plain living" of the area.

Their seventy-five-year-old clapboard store, with hardwood floors, a wood-burning stove, and an old-time cash register, carries sodas, candy, sandwich fixings, and Mrs. Plummer's homemade pecan, chocolate, and chess pies. In the back of the store, behind some chicken wire, there's a minimuseum of some thousand odds and ends that Mr.

Port Royal covered bridge over the Red River

Plummer has collected over the years. He walks by each relic, handles it with care, and tells the history of the item. In this quiet, small back room, lit only by a lightbulb hanging from the ceiling, Mr. Plummer is the history teacher and you are the pupil.

"What do you think this is?" he asks coyly, pointing to a foreign object. "It's what you use to take the heads off chickens." Mr. Plummer playfully gives the history of many items, including boxing gloves from 1922, an ice cruncher, a 112-year-old hat, an old-time fishing reel, and a 127-year-old apple peeler.

A practical joker, Mr. Plummer carves wooden gadgets, such as a three-piece chicken dinner—a wooden box with three kernels of corn inside. His eyes light up as he guides my husband toward a rock that reads, "Please turn me over." On the other side is written, "Thanks, that feels so much better."

The next stop along State 76 is Clarksville, the Montgomery County seat, a town filled with gorgeous antebellum homes and striking architecture. Founded in 1784, Clarksville was named for Revolutionary War hero George Rogers Clark.

One of the most architecturally interesting buildings is the Clarksville Montgomery County Museum, at 200 South 2nd Street. A majestic blend of Italianate ornamentation and Romanesque arches with classical eagles on the roof, the museum was constructed in 1898. It was designed by William M. Aiken, an architect who would later be appointed supervising architect by President Grover Cleveland.

One of the best small museums in the state, Clarksville Museum (open Tuesday through Sunday) includes items that explain the history of the area. The exhibits feature army uniforms and artifacts from the Civil War and both world wars, as well as displays of quilts, farming utensils, and Native American artifacts. The first floor of the museum focuses on the nineteenth century. Visitors walk over a wooden ramp

Clarksville Montgomery County Museum

and hear a church bell, a train whistle, and horse hooves and carriage wheels on a busy downtown street—all sounds of the past. The room is filled with old-time forms of transportation, ranging from carriages to a sled to an antique fire engine.

One display features an old schoolroom complete with desks, books, and school tablets. Another focuses on the homestead, with furniture, clothes, and dishes from the time. There are also old farming tools, such as a wheelbarrow, a tobacco hogshead, and a garden tractor. For the children, there's a hands-on explorer's room with a bubble exhibit, and Aunt Alice's Attic, filled with old toys and clothes.

Some of the other interesting architectural offerings in the area include the Immaculate Conception Roman Catholic Church, a classic Gothic-style building on the corner of Franklin and North 7th streets; Fifth Ward Baptist Church, an 1871 white brick building, at 900 Franklin Street, which served one of the earliest black congregations following the Civil War; and The Leaf Chronicle, a 1930s weathered red brick building housing Tennessee's oldest newspaper, founded in 1808.

Clarksville is also home to the Beachaven Vineyards and Winery, at 1100 Dunlop Lane. Sitting on about thirty-five acres, the winery grows almost three acres of French hybrid and American grapes on the property. They're harvested in August. A tour of Beachaven's wine- and champagne-making operation begins at the dock where the harvested grapes are brought in; the device in which the grapes' stems are removed and the grapes are crushed; the presser, where the grapes are squeezed; a fifty-eight-degree cave where the wine is stored in big tins; and the room used for storing fermenting champagne.

The winery offers tastings of all its products. Beachaven turns out some 15,000 gallons of wine and 480 gallons of champagne annually. Although some is sold in stores across Tennessee, most is sold on site. The gift shop also sells specialty cheeses, wine racks, and picnic baskets. There are picnic tables on the grounds for enjoying your purchases.

From Clarksville, take US 79 west to Dover, the Stewart County seat. Once an important source of iron ore, Dover had almost 800 inhabitants before the Civil War and was an important port on the Cumberland River.

The Fort Donelson National Battlefield, just across the river on US 79, tells the history of the North's first major victory of the Civil War, and the battle where Union Gen. Ulysses S. Grant got the nickname "Unconditional Surrender" Grant. Touring the ancient battlefield, you'll see the beautiful Cumberland River, where gunboats exchanged iron valentines on February 14, 1862. The Union soldiers had already captured Fort Henry, a port twelve miles upstream from Fort Donelson, but they suffered badly in the exchange on the water. While the Confederate soldiers celebrated victory, the Union soldiers, led by Gen. Ulysses S. Grant, surrounded the fort. Grant's counterattack pushed the Confederate soldiers farther and farther back. On the morning of February 16, Gen. Simon B. Buckner asked Grant for terms. Grant's famous reply, "No terms except an unconditional and immediate surrender can be accepted," has been entered in the chronicles of history.

Near the river lies what is left of the original fifteen-acre fort, built over a period of seven months by soldiers and slaves. More than a hundred huts stood at one time inside the fort's walls, made of logs and earth and standing ten feet tall. The huts were later burned by Union soldiers because of a measles epidemic.

The scenic roads are perfect for walking, driving, or riding bikes. Along the way, you'll see a Confederate monument commemorating the Southern soldiers who fought and died at Fort Donelson; parts of the fort; and the Dover Hotel, a structure built between 1851 and 1853 that served as General Buckner's headquarters. This is where Buckner surrendered some 13,000 Confederate soldiers to Grant; from here, the soldiers were loaded up and taken to Northern prisoner-of-war camps. The hotel, or Surrender House—open daily year-round—was refurbished in the 1970s and contains period furniture from the nineteenth century.

From Fort Donelson, take US 79 west a short way to TVA's Land Between the Lakes, a 170,000-acre reserve lying between Kentucky Lake and Lake Barkley. Look for the Trace, the southern entrance to the reserve.

Established in 1959 as an educational and recreational reserve, this area has an aquarium; a nature center with live animals, including a pair of red wolves; an observatory; the Homeplace, an 1850s interpretive history museum featuring Tennessee family life activities from that period; and a herd of about seventy buffalo that live in two 100-acre fields.

From the southern entrance of the reserve, the buffalo are only thirteen miles ahead on Trace Road. The speed limit along this pleasant, smooth drive is fifty miles per hour. You'll pass golden hay bales, green fields, and plenty of pickup trucks hauling fishing boats. The buffalo are hard to miss— they're surrounded by parked cars and camera-wielding people. The big brown animals graze noisily as adults ooh and aah and children try to lure the baby calves to the fence with shreds of grass. Seemingly accustomed to so much attention, the buffalo watch the onlookers with mild interest and continue eating grass. Several calves, with wobbly legs barely supporting their weight, were nursing. No threat of hunters. No threat of extinction. Just fields and fields of grass.

In the Area

Beachaven Vineyards and Winery (Clarksville):
615-645-8867

Bell Witch Village Antique Mall and the Bell Witch Opry (Adams): 615-696-2762, 696-2085

Clarksville Montgomery County Museum (Clarksville):
615-648-5780

Clarksville Montgomery County Tourist Commission
(Clarkesville): 615-648-0001

Fort Donelson National Battlefield and Cemetery (Dover):
615-232-5706

TVA's Land Between the Lakes (Dover):
615-232-7956

Plummer's Old Store Orchard and Museum (Clarksville):
615-358-9679

Port Royal (Covered Bridge) State Historic Site (Port Royal):
615-358-9696

9 ~

Union City

to

Trimble

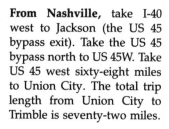

From Nashville, take I-40 west to Jackson (the US 45 bypass exit). Take the US 45 bypass north to US 45W. Take US 45 west sixty-eight miles to Union City. The total trip length from Union City to Trimble is seventy-two miles.

Highlights: *The bald eagles of Reelfoot Lake; Union City's Dixie Gun Works; Trimble's Independence Day Celebration; the quaint community of Ridgely; and the Dyer County Courthouse in Dyersburg.*

If you're an old gun enthusiast, you've probably heard of Dixie Gun Works—a prominent business in Union City. Even if you're not a gun enthusiast, you've probably heard of the films *Glory* and *The Last of the Mohicans*, movies filled with guns supplied by Dixie Gun Works.

"We sell a lot of guns and period clothing for reenacting events and for movies," says Hunter Kirkland, whose father, Turner Kirkland, founded the store. "And we have kits for guns, parts for repairing guns, supplies, leather goods, swords, tomahawks, real shooting cannons, period clothing, and tons of other things."

Turner Kirkland started collecting guns in 1931 when he was twelve. His father bought him an old Colt 1849 pocket model percussion revolver, and Kirkland loved it so much that his father continued to buy him antique guns. At the time, these guns cost between fifty cents and a dollar apiece. By the time Kirkland was seventeen, he and his father owned more than a hundred old guns.

In the 1950s, Turner Kirkland came back to his childhood love; he gave up his job as a salesman and opened a gun shop in an old coal shed. Today, that business is booming—selling about a thousand antique guns and 10,000 reproduction guns annually—in an establishment on Gun Powder Lane, just off US 51.

Dealing mostly in guns made before 1898, Dixie Gun Works has about a thousand antique revolvers and rifles on hand for sale at any given time. Some of the antique guns displayed in glass cases in the front of the store include a .58-caliber U.S. Springfield musket, one of the standard guns used during the Civil War; an 1860 Colt army revolver; an 1851 Colt navy revolver; a Miles pistol that was made for the Virginia Fourth Regiment before 1800; a Kentucky Penn rifle dating before 1800; and an English Matchlock rifle dating before 1600. The huge showroom is filled from floor to ceiling with displays of guns, gun parts, period costumes, ammunition—a smorgasbord for old-gun lovers.

Dixie Gun Works played a major role in the revival of interest in black powder, muzzle-loading guns, which were used up through the 1800s. In 1955, Turner Kirkland found a producer in Belgium to manufacture machine-made versions of these guns. Today, two of Dixie Gun Works' biggest sellers are the Kentucky long rifle and the Hawkins rifle, a big-bore gun that was popular with fur trappers, miners, and settlers in the 1800s.

Turner Kirkland also collects vintage cars. The Old Car Museum, which is housed in the Dixie Gun Works building, includes thirty-six cars, dating from 1908 to 1950. They're all restored, shiny, and in perfect working condition. The impressive collection includes a 1908 two-passenger Maxwell, a 1928 Victoria Studebaker, a 1916 Overland, a 1936 Packard limousine, a 1959 Edsel, and the pièce de résistance—a 1924 Marmon touring Car. Reagor Motlow, the last family president of the Jack Daniel Distillery, gave the car to Kirkland in 1961. Today it is worth more than $100,000.

The museum also includes seventy farm engines; a 1920 electric popcorn popper cart; a 1918 Harley Davidson motorcycle; an 1850 log gunshop with two rifling machines, a boring machine, and small tools; and literally thousands of antique car parts, such as headlights, electric horns, and motor meters.

Settled in 1854, Union City was named for the union of the railroads in this area. In 1890, it was voted the Obion County seat. The Obion County Museum, at 1004 Edwards Street, details the history of both Obion County and Union City. Opened in 1970, the museum features Native American artifacts, a Civil War display, a photographic display of the area, and a display of model railroads. A portion of the museum is a re-creation of "Main Street Yesterday," which includes a post office, barber shop, general store, print shop, and other businesses. The museum is open weekends only.

Several buildings and a monument in Union City are listed on the National Register of Historic Places. The Confederate Memorial, erected in 1869, is a white granite obelisk that rises forty feet into the air from the center of a cemetery on Edwards Street. The monument was the first of its kind to honor unknown Confederate dead.

From Union City, take State 22 west toward Tiptonville. On the way, you'll pass through Samburg, a small town filled with gift shops, such as Hillbilly Holler, where you can buy cans of freeze-dried Tennessee opossum.

Next stop—Tiptonville, home of Tennessee's *only* natural lake. Thousands of people come to this neck of the woods each year to fish, hunt, camp, and enjoy the wildlife of Reelfoot Lake.

More than 150 years ago, this fourteen-acre lake was relatively dry land. From December 16, 1811, to March 8, 1812, however, the New Madrid earthquakes, centered at nearby New Madrid, Missouri, shook the earth and changed the topographical features of northwest Tennessee. There was a series of 1,874 tremors, three of which are believed to be the strongest ever recorded in the United States. The tremors were felt over an area of a million square miles—as far away as Boston, Detroit, and New Orleans. The shaking climaxed on February 7, 1812, with what was probably the most violent earthquake ever to strike the North American continent. This whole land area sank as much as twenty feet, causing the waters of the Mississippi River to run backward for forty-eight hours, forming a lake filled with cypress and cottonwood trees. Few people were killed because the area, which was known then as (Chickasaw) "Indian country," was sparsely populated. Ornithologist and artist John James Audubon was there, however. He recorded, "The ground rose and fell in successive furrows, like the ruffled waters of a lake, and I became bewildered in my ideas, as I too plainly discovered that all this too awful commotion in nature was the result of an earthquake."

The lake gets its name from a Chickasaw warrior born with a clubfoot that caused him to "reel" as he walked. Named Kalopin, which meant "Reelfoot," the warrior became chief when his father died. According to Indian legend, the earthquakes were caused because the chieftain kidnapped a Choctaw princess, named Laughing Eyes, and took her as his bride. The gods punished Reelfoot with earthquakes that swallowed the warrior, his bride, and his entire tribe.

Chickasaw Indians used this area as hunting grounds until 1818, when they sold the land in the Jackson Purchase, which was designed by Andrew Jackson and Isaac Shelby. The purchased area included six million acres west of the Tennessee River from the Mississippi-Alabama line to the Ohio River. The Indians were given $15,000 a year for twenty years, which made this land worth about five cents an acre.

Today, Reelfoot Park is a 25,000-acre haven for 253 species of birds and many kinds of animals, including mink, white-tailed deer, and raccoons. The 12,000-acre Reelfoot Lake holds some fifty-eight species of fish—about 500 pounds of fish per acre. The most plentiful is crappie, a bony but delicious fish that can be found on most restaurant menus around the lake.

The underwater roots of the cypress trees in Reelfoot Lake form a natural fish hatchery unsurpassed in the world. An abundance of fish and mild, ice-free winters make Reelfoot a great vacation spot for birds of prey, such as bald eagles, whose diet is about 90 percent fish. On a slow day, eagles settle for rabbits, coots, or injured waterfowl. In early November, the bald eagles leave their summer homes around the Great Lakes and Canada to come to Reelfoot, where they stay until about mid-March. As many as 200 bald eagles, the highest concentration in Tennessee, can be found in the peak months of January and February.

About 12,000 people come to the lake each year to see our nation's symbol in action. From December 1 to March 10, Reelfoot Park offers daily eagle tours by bus, beginning at the Airpark Inn off State 78 (901-253-7756). These tours are popular, so be sure to make reservations. The two-hour tour includes the history of Dyer, Obion, and Lake counties, as well as a search for eagles. It passes Tiptonville Dome—the highest point in Lake County—a nine-foot rise that is the only wrinkle in the flat landscape besides the man-made levees that hold back the Mississippi River.

Whenever park ranger James Cox spotted a black blob in the trees on the day we took the tour, he parked the bus and set up a telescope for the visitors to use. The bird was usually too far away to see with the naked eye, but with a telescope or binoculars, we could distinguish the regal bird's dark body and white head.

"Benjamin Franklin didn't want the bald eagle to be the national symbol because it makes its living off other birds," Cox says. "He thought we should have chosen the wild turkey. But I think the bald eagle has some redeeming qualities, too. It's a powerful bird and it's found only in North America. I think our forefathers did a good job of choosing it as our national symbol."

The nation's symbol since 1782, the bird gets its name from an old English word, *Bbalde,* which means "white." When eagles fly, their powerful wings spread six to eight feet, carrying them an average of thirty-six to forty-four miles an hour. A bald eagle weighs ten to twelve pounds.

The tour includes a visit to the Reelfoot Lake Visitor Center, in Buford Ellington Hall, a museum featuring catfish, turtles, red milk and cottonmouth snakes, rattlesnakes, and king snakes—all indigenous to the area. There are also exhibits about the history of the area, and an earthquake simulator. An enormous outdoor cage houses bald eagles that could not survive in the wild. One eagle was missing a leg and the other one suffered a brain injury because of exposure to pesticides.

Other birds that can be spotted throughout the year include red-tailed hawks, red-shouldered hawks, northern harriers, osprey, American kestrels, barred owls, great horned owls, and common screech owls. More than 250,000 ducks and 50,000 Canada geese winter at Reelfoot. Watching thousands of ducks and Canada geese lift off the water—the whites and silvers of their bodies and wings reflecting the early-morning sun—was absolutely breathtaking.

Any time of year is a good one to visit Reelfoot Lake. But be warned. Scientists say that powerful earthquakes happened here before 1811 and the big ones are believed to happen every 600 years. So you might want to come before the year 2411.

From Tiptonville, take State 78 south to Dyersburg. The road is not the most scenic, but the destination is worth the trip. The Dyer County seat, Dyersburg is one of the biggest cities in northwest Tennessee, with 18,500 people. It's located on a bluff that was formerly known as McIver's Grant. Joel H. Dyer at one time owned the 640-acre tract and then donated it to create the town, which was originally chartered in 1850.

The red brick Dyer County Courthouse is one of the prettier ones in the state. It's the sixth courthouse to be built on the site: this one has been standing since 1912 and is listed on the National Register of Historic Places. Dyersburg's Veterans Square is lined with family-owned businesses.

If you're interested in bicycling, there's a scenic bike route on low-traffic roads from Dyer County to Reelfoot Lake. For information call the Dyer County Chamber of Commerce at 901-285-3433.

One of the town's biggest events is the Dogwood Dash, a five-kilometer and ten-kilometer run held in April. The Dogwood Festival, which is held in conjunction with the race, includes a parade, arts and crafts, storytelling, food, children's games, a street dance, live music, and all-around fun.

From Dyersburg, take State 211 north to Newbern. The big news in this small town is the Newbern Train Depot. Built in 1929, the depot was recently listed on the National Register of Historic Places. After the depot was restored, Amtrak changed its New Orleans to Chicago route so that it stops in Newbern instead of Dyersburg.

"Since April of 1992, more than 3,000 people have caught the train here," says Joe Adams, the mayor of Newbern. "Of course, now that the depot is on the National Register, people come to see it, too."

A charming, red brick building with green and yellow trim around the windows, the depot faces Newbern's Main Street, a quiet place with almost no traffic. "Newbern was founded in the early 1850s," says Adams, a Newbern native. "It used to be a real cotton center, and that's why the railroad was so important. Newbern started out as a small village and now it's a big village."

From Newbern, take State 211 north to Trimble, then head east on County 105 for less than a mile to Main Street. Just look for a row of century-old buildings, all connected like Lego blocks.

Jesse Pierce is considered the founder of Trimble because he donated the original five acres for the town. It was named, however, for Judge John Trimble, the person responsible for the legislation that brought the railroad to Trimble. The town was incorporated in 1873.

Trimble, at its earliest, was a sawmill town with little law and order—the kind of town where mothers, children, and law-abiding citizens stayed indoors at night. There was a drugstore, a one-room schoolhouse, a post office, four small churches, a blacksmith shop, four general stores, two hotels, a boardinghouse, a livery stable, a water trough, a hitching rack, and four saloons.

Today, everything that happens in the small town of about 700 people happens on Main Street. And the big Fourth of July Festival is no exception. The town's biggest holiday includes a parade, homemade ice cream, singing, a band, a dance, fireworks, and the annual cakewalk. Trimble is so serious about the "sweet" event that they've painted an official cakewalk circle with boxes numbered from one to thirty-four in the middle of Main Street.

In the Area

Dixie Gun Works and The Old Car Museum (Union City): 901-885-0700

Dyersburg/Dyer County Chamber of Commerce (Dyersburg): 901-285-3433

Newbern City Hall (Newbern): 901-627-3221

Obion County Chamber of Commerce (Union City): 901-885-0211

Obion County Museum (Union City): 901-885-6774, 901-885-1539

Reelfoot Lake (Tiptonville): 901-538-2481

Reelfoot Lake Air Park Inn (Tiptonville): 901-253-7756

Reelfoot Lake Visitor Center, Buford Ellington Hall (Tiptonville): 901-253-9652

Sportsman's Resort (Tiptonville): 901-253-6581

Trimble Library (Trimble): 901-297-2702

10 ~

Memphis

to

Shiloh

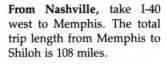

From Nashville, take I-40 west to Memphis. The total trip length from Memphis to Shiloh is 108 miles.

Highlights: _The musical history of Graceland and Sun Studio, the appeal of Beale Street, and the step-back-in-time feel of A. Schwab's Dry Goods Store, all in Memphis; the antebellum homes of La Grange; and the bloody battle of Shiloh depicted in the Shiloh National Military Park._

Traveling east from Memphis to Shiloh is one continuous barbecue and blues fest, from the live music of Beale Street in Memphis to the backwoods "cue" places along the way. There's plenty of food and history to be found in the hundred-mile stretch between the sprawling river metropolis of Memphis and the rolling hills of Shiloh, where one of the bloodiest battles of the Civil War was fought.

Memphis, the oldest city in Shelby County and the biggest city in Tennessee, offers everything from the blues of Beale Street to the posh Peabody Hotel to Elvis's house. This is the city where the King of rock 'n' roll made his first recording. More than 650,000 people visit the city annually to see Graceland, Presley's fourteen-acre estate at 3675 Elvis Presley Boulevard.. The lines can be long, especially during the summer. Tours are offered every five minutes, and reservations are suggested. Before 11:00 A.M. and after 3:00 P.M. are the best times to visit during the summer. Tours are not very crowded in the fall.

Opened in 1982, five years after Presley's death, the twenty-three-room mansion cost the musical giant $100,000 in 1957. The tour offers a look at six rooms, all complete with at least one TV; a grand piano covered in 24-carat gold leaf; and a Trophy Room that showcases his twenty-year career. Presley made 650 recordings and thirty-three motion pictures and sold more than one billion records worldwide.

Elvis's toys include Harley Davidson motorcycles, a 1956 purple Cadillac convertible, the 1955 pink Cadillac that Elvis bought for his mother, two sleek black Stutz Blackhawks, a huge Convair 880 jet named *Lisa Marie,* and a ten-seat Lockheed Jetstar named *Hound Dog II.*

The house gives you a feel for the man. A native of Tupelo, Mississippi, Elvis was a humble, religious, different kind of guy who loved his mother. Sun Studio, the site of Elvis's first recording in 1954, gives you a feel for his music. Owned and operated by Sam C. Phillips in the late 1950s, the legendary Sun Studio, at 706 Union Avenue, launched the careers of performers such as Elvis, Jerry Lee Lewis, Carl Perkins, Johnny Cash, Roy Orbison, Rufus Thomas, and Charlie Rich.

You can get grilled food, sandwiches, and hot coffee at the hip Sun Studio Cafe next door. In the 1950s, this restaurant was called Mrs. Taylor's, named for its owner. Supposedly many a Sun Record Label contract was signed here.

Ned Lathrop led our Sun Studio tour of three people. A true-blue Elvis fan, Lathrop moved to Memphis *just* to be near the King. "I was an Elvis fan," says Lathrop, a twenty-something native of Wisconsin. "That's why I came here. I started washing dishes in the restaurant and worked up to tour guide. Now I get to play Elvis all day and spread the gospel."

Lathrop, who has virtually memorized Presley's life story, takes us into the small three-room studio where Orbison, Lewis, Perkins, Cash, Presley, and, in recent years, the Irish rock band U2 have made recording history. Huge black-and-white photos of the artists and framed records line the walls. The entire thirty-minute tour takes place in the main room. Visitors stand and listen to music bits and play-by-play histories of the people who made this little Memphis recording studio famous. Lathrop uses a disc jockey–style delivery to announce the music clips, like Elvis's famous "My Happiness" and "That's Where Your Heartaches Begin."

Although the building has served as a studio, a barber shop, a radiator repair shop, and a garage for storage over the years, the floor and the acoustic tiles on the ceiling have never been altered. "A lot of people record here because of the sound," Lathrop says. "With this funky ceiling, the sound bounces all over the place."

Before rock 'n' roll took the country by storm, there was another sound in Memphis—a raw, sultry sound called the blues. The music hit its heyday in the 1920s and 1930s in the entertainment district known as Beale Street. At that time, Memphis was the center of black commerce and entertainment and a mecca for musicians such as Rufus Thomas, Louis Armstrong, Bobby Blue Band, Johnny Ace, and "The Beale Street Blues Boy," better known as B. B. King.

William Christopher (W. C.) Handy, the "Father of the Blues," is the man credited with bringing blues into the mainstream. Writing down the music he had heard in the cotton fields and honky-tonks, Handy generated some of the greats such as "The St. Louis Blues" and "The Beale Street Blues." A bronze statue of Handy holding his trumpet still stands in Handy Park, which is on the corner of Third and Beale streets.

W. C. Handy still overlooks his beloved Beale Street

New nightclubs, such as Carl Perkins' Blue Suede Shoes Club, the Rum Boogie Cafe, and B. B. King's Blues Club, line Beale Street now. It's still the place to be at night—three blocks of live music, great food, and blues blasting through speakers on the street.

"If you can't find it here, you don't need it" is the slogan of A. Schwab's Dry Goods Store, at 163 Beale Street. Currently owned by Abram Schwab, the store was started by his grandfather in 1876. It sells everything from ladies' bloomers to men's garters to extra-large clothes—up to the eighties in pants and up to size seventeen in shoes. There are hats, wool socks, sewing notions and fabric, a line of voodoo supplies, love potions, and more than a thousand ties. "We've got regular customers because we've got things no one else carries—things that are difficult to find," says Schwab. "As you get older, style doesn't mean as much to you. So when grandma says to get her some cotton stockings at Schwab's, you better get her those stockings or she'll hit you over the head with her cane."

Schwab loves his store, but his true passion is A. Schwab's Beale Street Museum, which is housed upstairs. The sixty-nine-year-old Memphis native collects items that tell the history of Beale Street and the Mississippi River Delta country. Rusted farm tools, picture books, antique clothing, and other gadgets line the shelves. Ask Schwab about them—he loves sharing the history of his neighborhood.

Of course his museum doesn't go back to Beale Street's beginning in 1841. During the Civil War, the street served as headquarters for Gen. Ulysses S. Grant. The street had its heyday in the 1920s, when it took on a carnival atmosphere of gambling, drinking, prostitution, voodoo, murder, and booming nightclubs. During the Great Depression, a local tailor by the name of Louis Lettes designed the Zoot Suit —a trademark of the era. Today, Beale Street's business is not quite so shady. There are restaurants, the Chamber of

Commerce, the New Daisy Theater, and plenty of street vendors selling T-shirts and other memorabilia.

Any visit to Memphis should include ducks and ribs—that's the Peabody Hotel's ducks, and the Rendezvous' ribs. Located within a few blocks of each other, they're Memphis mainstays and well worth a visit.

The original Peabody Hotel opened in 1869 during the Reconstruction years. The showplace hotel had seventy-five rooms, private baths, and a ballroom. Some of the guests who frequented the Peabody included Presidents Andrew Johnson and William McKinley, Confederate Gen. Robert E. Lee, and William Faulkner. The restored Peabody, at 149 Union Avenue, opened in 1981 with larger rooms, a Grecian-style swimming pool in the basement, and many of the original features, such as the stained glass skylights in the lobby and the ducks.

The first ducks moved in around 1930 when Frank Schutt was the hotel's general manager. An avid hunter who used real duck decoys, Schutt and his friends decided to house the decoy ducks in the hotel lobby's travertine marble fountain. It's been a tradition ever since. The current residents—a mallard drake and four hens—reside on the Peabody roof in "The Duck Palace." Each day at 11:00 A.M., the ducks are escorted by a bellman down to the lobby for "The Duck Ceremony," in which they waddle regally over a newly rolled red carpet to the strains of "The King Cotton March." They swim in the fountain all day, then at 5:00 P.M. they reverse the parade and walk back on a red carpet to the elevator and up to their penthouse suite. The entire ceremony takes about ten minutes, but you should get there early because people flock to see the feathered parade. A bird's-eye view is best: take the elevator up to the second floor and stand along the railing overlooking the fountain.

Near the Peabody Hotel are the Delta Ducks. You can't miss these huge contraptions—they look like big white boats on wheels. Built in 1943, a duck is a U.S. Army amphibious vehicle so named because of its secret code designation during World War II, DUKW. The thirty-one-foot-long vehicles take visitors on a unique tour—down the streets of Memphis and *on* the Wolf River to Mud Island. The hour-long tours begin at Duck Port, between the Radisson and Peabody hotels, at 185 Union Avenue. Other stops along the way include Confederate Park, Riverside Drive, and Beale Street.

The Rendezvous, 52 South 2nd Street, near the Peabody Hotel, *does* ribs. Here since 1948, the restaurant serves charcoal-broiled dry ribs that are some of the best in the state. The no-frills restaurant offers sandwiches, chicken, lamb, and salads, but for us, eating anything but ribs would be like ordering a hamburger at a seafood restaurant.

Besides the food, you'll enjoy the atmosphere at Rendezvous. It has the feel of a family barbecue—red-and-white checkered tablecloths and plenty of friendly servers. The walls are lined with antiques and memorabilia—oil paintings, firearms, and old photographs. If you don't have time to eat at the Rendezvous, you can have their ribs sent to your home. They deliver anywhere in the continental United States.

If you want great barbecue sandwiches, follow the Memphis natives to Payne's Barbq, at 1762 Lamar Avenue. Housed in a renovated service station, the restaurant offers succulent barbecue on traditional white bread, ribs, potato chips, and cole slaw. Drinks come from the vending machine and there are a few tables and chairs in the former car repair shop. Open since 1972, the restaurant has a faithful following. When we were there—at 3:00 P.M. on a weekday—there was a line, and there were about six cars in the parking lot, including a beat-up old Ford pickup truck and a BMW with Texas tags.

Burke's Bookstore, at 1719 Poplar Avenue, has been open since 1875. It's a great place to get lost for hours. Offering new and used books, the comfortably laid-out store specializes in southern authors, Civil War, and black history first editions.

The store hosts several authors each month and mails quarterly newsletters to people across the United States.

Other attractions in Memphis include the Memphis Brooks Museum of Art, 1905 Overton Park Avenue; The Orpheum Theatre, 203 South Main Street; The Memphis Pink Palace Museum, 3050 Central Avenue; the Lichterman Nature Center, 5992 Quince Road; The Pyramid, One Auction Avenue; The Children's Museum of Memphis, 2525 Central Avenue; and The National Civil Rights Museum in the Lorraine Motel, 450 Mulberry Street, where Dr. Martin Luther King, Jr., was killed on April 4, 1968. The Memphis Cook Convention Center, 255 North Main Street, offers worldrenowned traveling exhibits, such as "Catherine the Great" and "Napoleon."

Billed as "America's largest festival," Memphis in May includes more than a hundred events such as music, dance, theater, sports, visual arts, and a World Championship Barbecue Cooking Contest with a $25,000 purse. There's also the Beale Street Music Festival, which is held in Beale Street nightclubs and in W. C. Handy Park.

Take Poplar Avenue east out of Memphis to go to Germantown. The six-lane road takes you past the Memphis Brooks Museum of Art and Overton Park (mentioned above) and a beautiful residential area. Poplar Avenue becomes State 57/US 72 in Germantown, the tenth largest city in the state. In its early days, Germantown was known as Pea Ridge. It lies on a ridge of land separating the watershed of the Wolf River on the north from that of Nonconnah Creek to the south. This was originally the land of the Chickasaw Indians. In 1825 Frances Wright, an idealistic reformer, established a commune called "Nashoba," which is the Indian word for "wolf." Her intent was to use the area to educate slaves and then free them, but she didn't get much support and the commune finally closed.

Soon after this, settlers began moving in. No one knows for sure where Germantown got its name—possibly from the town's huge German immigrant population, or a railroad surveyor whose last name was German, or the German-born innkeeper Mr. Luchen. The name of the town was changed temporarily to Nashoba during World War I because of a growing anti-German sentiment, but it was changed back to Germantown after the war.

The town was incorporated in 1841; the Memphis and Charleston Railroad opened here in 1852. In 1950 there were only 400 people; today there are about 40,000. It's a "bedroom community" with a lot of charm and many parks. Supposedly, there is a park within a half mile of every resident.

The heart of the community lies at the corner of Poplar Pike and Germantown Road, where you'll find the Germantown Depot. Built in 1852 as a stop for the Memphis and Charleston Railroad, the depot now houses a collection of railroad memorabilia.

One of Germantown's best offerings is the Germantown Commissary, a barbecue place just across the way from the depot. Walker Taylor III ran a grocery on these grounds in a building that was built around the turn of the century. One Saturday afternoon in 1974, Taylor was running the grocery store while barbecuing a pork shoulder outside for company that night. It smelled so good that a store customer offered to buy it right off the grill for a good sum—enough for Taylor to take his company out to dinner anyway. So Taylor sold the pork and the next Saturday, he barbecued five shoulders. Pretty soon, the store turned into a barbecue restaurant.

Taylor's son, Walker Taylor IV, still serves the same finger-licking, hickory-smoked, lightly glazed barbecue and ribs. The recipes are originals, even though the building is semi-new. "The original building served as a doctor's office, then a grocery store, and then a restaurant," Taylor says. "But one day we got carried away cooking and burned the place down. So we built this restaurant in 1984."

From Germantown, take US 72 east to Collierville. First known as Oak Grove, the town was actually once part of both Tennessee and Mississippi due to a surveyor's three-mile-plus error, but it was corrected in 1838. Collierville, which is the second-oldest town in Shelby County, gets its name from Jesse R. Collier.

The first Collierville was incorporated in 1850 east of its present site. During the Civil War, however, Collierville's buildings were burned to the ground during a battle between the Union and Confederate soldiers. Harrison Irby and Virginus Leake bought about ninety acres of the present location in 1867 and the second Colliersville was incorporated in 1870, about the time the square was born.

Collierville was struck by tragedy again in the 1870s with a fatal epidemic of yellow fever. Many people from Collierville and Memphis who were killed by the fever are buried in Magnolia Cemetery on Mount Pleasant Road. Tombstones from the mid-1800s to the present line the large cemetery, which is shaded by magnolia trees. In the historic section, you'll find a summer house and a stone chapel that was restored recently by a local Boy Scout troop.

Collierville is known for its downtown square, which is on the National Register of Historic Places. Some of the turn-of-the-century buildings in the quaint quadrangle include The Collierville Antique Mall, which was built in 1916 and originally housed both the Kelsey Brothers Mercantile Store and the local telephone exchange; the Shepherd Building, which was built in 1890 and served as a local grocery store; and St. Andrews Episcopal Church, a beautiful Gothic Revival design built in 1890 and located one block off the square on Walnut Street.

A train car and engine dating back to the early twentieth century stand like beacons to the past on tracks south of the square. "The Savannah," an executive railcar built in 1915, offers an observation room, a valet's room, two suites, a dining room, and a stainless steel kitchen with crew's quarters. The engine "No. 1351" was built in 1912 for the Frisco railroad and weighs about 230 tons. During World War II, this old train engine pulled troop trains; it was retired in 1952. Tours of the antique railcar and engine are offered Wednesdays and the first Saturday of each month and by appointment through Main Street Collierville (901-853-1666). Main Street, which is located on the square, also offers maps of historic downtown walking tours.

Collierville's main festival, Fair on the Square, is held the first weekend in May in the town square. It draws some 10,000 visitors to the little town of 16,000. A heartwarming slice of Americana, the family event includes vendors of everything from cotton candy to crafts, plus children's activities and clowns.

LaGrange, about twenty-five miles east on State 57, is the oldest town in Fayette County, which was named for Marquis de Lafayette for his contribution to America's fight for independence. LaGrange gets its name from Lafayette's country estate in France.

The now quiet little town used to be *the* place to be. Nestled along a 300-foot bluff overlooking the Wolf River, the area was originally a trading post, known as the "Cluster of Pines" before the Native Americans were forcefully removed. By the time LaGrange was incorporated in 1836, it was a thriving settlement. Gradually, "La Belle Village," as it was also known, developed into a commercial center and became known throughout the state as a center of culture, wealth, society, and education. At the time, nearby Memphis was thought of as a rough, rowdy river town.

One of LaGrange's most famous citizens at the time was Lucy Holcombe Pickens, "Queen of the Confederacy." Born in 1832, Holcombe grew up in La Grange and eventually married South Carolina congressman Francis W. Pickens. When her husband served as the governor of the Confederate state of South Carolina, her image was put on the Confederate $1 note and was later placed on three different $100 Confederate notes. She was the only woman to be so honored by the Confederate States of America.

By the 1850s, LaGrange had four churches, two colleges, two newspapers, blacksmiths, gunsmiths, bakers, dress shops, jewelry stores, drugstores, dry goods stores, hotels, and dentists' offices, as well as a post office and a train depot. All of that changed, however, with the Civil War, when federal troops occupied the area. Forty-five of the town's homes were burned, and gardens were trampled. Most of the remaining buildings, such as the town's schools and churches, were used as hospitals for wounded soldiers.

LaGrange never recovered, but you can still see some of the town's original grandeur in many of the remaining original antebellum homes. The entire community is on the National Register of Historic Places. Woodlawn, a two-story white Colonial home built in 1828, is probably the most magnificent in the area. It was built by Maj. Charles Michie, a veteran of the War of 1812, who possessed a land warrant for his military services. When the Union troops occupied La Grange in 1862, Woodlawn became the west Tennessee headquarters for Gen. William T. Sherman. Located on State 57, the historic home has nine large rooms, each with a fireplace.

LaGrange is also home to one of the oldest churches in Tennessee, the Immanuel Episcopal Church, which was built in 1842. The English Country–style church, located on Second Street off State 57, was used as a hospital and barracks during the Civil War.

Cogbill's Store and Museum, which was established in the late 1860s, still stands. The original general merchandise store, which was opened by William Peter Lipscomb, was destroyed in a tornado in 1900. In 1901, Lipscomb rebuilt the store that stands today. His daughter, Sallie Lipscomb, and her husband, Edmond Taylor Cogbill, inherited the store and then passed it on to their son, Charles Lipscomb Cogbill, who ran the store until his death in 1964.

Located at the intersection of LaGrange Road and State 57, the store used to sell hardware, groceries, salted meats, medicine, and tonics. Reopened in 1991 by Sherri Bruner-Osteen and Lucy Cogbill, granddaughter of the original founder, the store, with old wooden floorboards, sells everything from hand-crocheted doilies to pottery to handmade jewelry to antiques.

Many of the area's historic private homes and churches are opened annually for the Architectural Treasures of Fayette County Tour, which is held in October. For information on the event, call the Fayette County Chamber of Commerce at 901-465-8690.

From LaGrange, take State 57 east to Grand Junction, home of the 18,500-acre Ames Plantation. Located on Buford Ellington Road, the estate is the site of the National Field Trial Championship, which is held each year in February. Dubbed the "world series for bird dogs," the eight- to ten-day event draws people from across the United States.

The first National Field Trial Championship was held in West Point, Mississippi, in 1896, but the event moved to Grand Junction in 1900. Hobart Ames, former owner of the Ames Plantation, served as president of the National Field Trial Champion Association for forty-three years and helped establish the guidelines for judging the best of the bird dogs—guidelines that are still used today. During the time he served as president, the Ames Plantation became synonymous with the field trials.

Because of strict guidelines, only about thirty to forty dogs in the country are accepted into the grueling competition. The dogs are required to compete for three hours at a time, running through thickets, sand, ditches, and creeks—rain or shine, in sleet or snow.

Riding horses, the judges follow the dogs. "The dog must have a great bird sense," Hobart Ames stipulated in the original rules. Besides their bird sense, the dogs are also judged for their speed, range, style, character, and ability to find and point quail.

If you're more interested in history than the hunt, the Manor House or Cedar Grove, which is located on the Ames Plantation, is a wonderful old home to visit. The original portion of the southern Federal-style manor was begun in 1847 by John Walker Jones. Hobart Ames purchased the house in 1901 and added a two-story wing for his servants and all of the amenities he had enjoyed in his home near Boston, Massachusetts. The house is open for touring the fourth Thursday of each month from March through October.

Grand Junction's National Bird Dog Museum and Field Trial Hall of Fame pays homage to the top dogs of this century. Created by the Bird Dog Foundation, the museum includes photographs, video film footage, paintings, and histories of prize pointers. An arresting and intriguing bronze statue of a man hunting with his dog stands outside the museum, which is located on State 57.

From Grand Junction, take State 57 east to Michie, then State 22 north to the Shiloh National Military Park. This is the land of cotton—there are acres of the white stuff around here. As you approach the park, you'll begin to see battlefield monuments along the sides of the road.

Manse George's Cabin at Shiloh

Shiloh was one of the first four national military parks to be established between 1890 and 1899. The pristine park of 3,800 acres remains untouched. A tour of Shiloh should begin with the twenty-five-minute Civil War reenactment film, which brings to life the first major battle of the Civil War fought in the West. The museum includes cannons, haversacks, swords, surgeon's equipment, provisions for war, uniforms, and a display of the makeshift hospital that was set up at Shiloh. It was the first known military field hospital.

You can take a self-guided tour or an auto narrative tape tour. The two-lane concrete roads are great for bike riding, driving, or walking. The tours begin at Pittsburgh Landing on the Tennessee River and include sites such as the Hornets'

Nest, the Confederate burial trench, Johnston's death site, and the Bloody Pond, where wounded from both sides came to drink, bathe their wounds, and die. The battle is commemorated with 152 monuments and 475 historical, camp, and troop position iron tablets.

The stage was set for the Battle of Shiloh in February 1862 after Union forces, under the leadership of Gen. Ulysses S. Grant, had captured Fort Henry and Fort Donelson, formerly controlled by the Confederates. As a result, Gen. Albert Sidney Johnston took his troops and withdrew to Corinth, Mississippi, where he joined Generals Beauregard, Bragg, and Polk.

Meanwhile, the Union army moved up the Tennessee River to Pittsburgh Landing and occupied "Camp Shiloh." They waited at Shiloh, which was named for a log meetinghouse near the camp, for the arrival of Gen. Don Carlos Buell. With Buell's 25,000 men, Grant would be able to beat Johnston's army.

Johnston had plans of his own—a surprise attack with his 40,000 men on Grant at Shiloh before Buell could get there. Johnston and his men set out on April 3 for a twenty-mile march to Shiloh. On the night of April 5, the two great armies slept within gunshot range of each other.

The Confederate army launched an attack at dawn the next morning and the fighting lasted into the night. The surprised Union forces retreated to an old sunken road, a natural line of defense, while the Confederates launched a sixty-two-cannon bombardment that literally blew the line to pieces. You can easily imagine Confederate soldiers next to the trees on the far side of an unspoiled field firing cannonballs at the Union soldiers in a sunken area to the left.

The Union army retreated to the river, where they spent the night and were joined by General Buell's army the next morning. General Johnston, the highest-ranking officer killed in battle during the entire war, died the day before, after taking a minié ball in the knee that severed a main artery.

On April 7, General Grant led his army of 54,000 to victory over the Confederate soldiers, who were now being led by General Beauregard. By the end of the day, Beauregard called for a general retreat, and the Union soldiers didn't follow.

During the tour, you'll see the 300-yard expanse where the Confederate soldiers shot sixty-two cannons—the largest use of artillery on the American continent up to that point. There are also plenty of large, marble monuments, most of them dedicated to Union soldiers. The Confederate soldiers were buried in two common areas, piled one on top of another. More than 23,000 soldiers were killed on these grounds during "Bloody Shiloh."

Nearby Hagy's Catfish Hotel is also intertwined with the Civil War. The place was originally settled by Henry and Polly Hagy when they docked their flatboat here on the Tennessee River in 1825. They built a farm, which their son, John Hagy, eventually inherited. John built a log shack, which was later occupied by Union soldiers and eventually destroyed.

Then the place got the nickname of "Catfish Hotel" when relative Norvin Hagy entertained friends at cookouts. Because the river wasn't safe to travel at night, many of his friends had to spend the night, thus the name.

In 1938, Norvin Hagy was prompted to open a restaurant, which was an immediate success. A fire in 1975 destroyed the original structure; the present restaurant was built a year later. A third generation of Hagys runs the business now, making it one of the oldest family-owned restaurants in the country.

The entrance to the restaurant is on Cotton Landing Road, just 500 feet north of the entrance to Shiloh National Military Park along State 22. Just watch for a huge gray Ferris wheel, covered with kudzu. Lost in time, the huge contraption was originally part of an old amusement park. Now it's just a handy landmark.

Overlooking the Tennessee River, the casual restaurant serves catfish that's lightly coated and fried to perfection. The fish is fresh and the hush puppies are excellent.

For an interesting detour, take State 22 north, then US 64 west to Adamsville, home of the former Buford Pusser, McNairy County's most famous citizen.

"I knew him in high school," says Martha Tucker, a museum hostess and native of Adamsville. "He was a very quiet, well-mannered young man. All of the teachers loved him, and if he talked to someone who was older, he always said, 'Sir' and 'Ma'am.' "

After high school, Pusser became a professional wrestler and later served as chief of police. At the age of twenty-six, he became the sheriff of McNairy County—the youngest man to be elected sheriff in Tennessee.

Pusser was the Arnold Schwarzenegger of law enforcement. During his three terms in office, from 1964 to 1970, he made a lot of enemies by closing down eighty-seven illegal whiskey stills and cleaning up gambling and prostitution rings. As a result, Pusser was shot eight times and knifed seven times. He once fought off six men, sending three to the hospital and the other three to jail; he also killed two people in self-defense. He was gunned down in an ambush on August 12, 1967, which killed his wife, Pauline, and left him with severe facial injuries. The legendary lawman was finally killed in a flaming 1974 automobile crash that was *supposedly* an accident.

You can see the large brick house where Pusser, whose life was the basis of the *Walking Tall* movies, lived with his wife and three children. It includes family photographs and newspaper and magazine clippings that detail his bloody encounters and a twenty-minute film featuring Dwana, the Pussers' youngest daughter, talking about her family.

For safety's sake, Pusser turned his house into a small fortress. The garage is enclosed inside the house; there's an alarm system on every door; and there are no windows in the master bedroom.

"After he was sheriff, they unanimously elected him constable so he could carry a firearm with him at all times," says museum hostess Martha Tucker. "He had it with him when he was killed. I say, 'killed' because I believe he was killed. They just never proved it. I don't know who did it. I just know it was the 'bad guys.' "

In the Area

Ames Plantation (Grand Junction): 901-465-8690, 901-878-1067

Burke's Bookstore (Memphis): 901-278-7484

Cogbill's Store and Museum (LaGrange): 901-878-1235

The Delta Ducks (Memphis): 901-527-6823

Fayette County Chamber of Commerce (Somerville): 901-465-8690

Germantown Commissary (Germantown): 901-754-5540

Germantown Depot (Germantown): 901-755-1200

Graceland (Memphis): 800-238-2000

Hagy's Catfish Hotel (Shiloh): 901-689-3327

Main Street (Collierville): 901-853-1666

Payne's Barbq (Memphis): 901-942-7433

The Peabody Hotel (Memphis): 901-529-4000

Buford Pusser Home and Museum (Adamsville): 901-632-4080

Rendezvous (Memphis): 901-523-2746

A. Schwab's Dry Goods Store (Memphis):
901-523-9782

Shiloh National Military Park (Shiloh):
901-689-5275

Sun Studio (Memphis): 901-521-0664

mississippi River PARK.(memphis)

Index

Index

Index

Index

National Civil Rights Museum, Memphis, 142

New Bethel Baptist Church, Oak Ridge, 48

Obion County Museum, Union City, 128

Old Car Museum, Union City, 127–128

Old Jail Museum, Winchester, 5

The Parthenon, Nashville, 98–99

Plummer's Old Store Orchard and Museum, Clarksville, 118–120

Bufurd Pusser Home and Museum, Adamsville, 152–153

Red Clay Museum, Cleveland, 17, 74

Reelfoot Lake Visitor Center, Tiptonville, 131

Rhea County Courthouse, Dayton, 71–72

Rocky Mount, Piney Flats, 36–37

Sequoyah Birthplace Museum, Vonore, 79

Shiloh National Military Park, Shiloh, 148–151

South Cumberland State Park Visitor Center, Tracy City, 10

Sycamore Shoals State Historic Area, Elizabethton, 37–38

Tipton-Haynes Historical Farm, Johnson City, 35

Van Vechten Gallery, Nashville, 105

James White Fort, Knoxville, 41

LODGING. *See* INNS and LODGING

MILLS. *See* BAKERIES, CANNERIES, DISTILLERIES, FACTORIES, MILLS and WINERIES

MINERAL WATERS and MINES

Armour's Red Boiling Springs Hotel, Red Boiling Springs, 84, 86

Coker Creek Falls, Coker Creek, 78

Craighead Caverns, Sweetwater, 79–80

Ducktown Basin Museum, Ducktown, 77

Palace Park, Red Boiling Springs, 86

MUSEUMS. *See* LIVING HISTORY SITES and MUSEUMS

MUSIC HALLS. *See* AMUSEMENT PARKS, MUSIC HALLS and THEATERSOUTDOOR RECREATION. *See* PARKS and OUTDOOR RECREATION

PARKS and OUTDOOR RECREATION

Bandy Creek Horse Stables, Allardt, 54

Big South fork National River and Recreation Area, Allardt, 53–54

Burgess Falls State Natural Area, Cookeville, 93

Centennial Park, Nashville, 99

Cherokee National Forest, Ocoee, 75–76

Chickamauga National Military Park, Chattanooga, 19

Colditz Cove State Natural Area, Allardt, 54

Craighead Caverns, Sweetwater, 79–80

Davy Crockett Birthplace State Park, Limestone, 29

David Crockett State Park, Lawrenceburg, 112

Dale Hollow Lake, Celina, 90

Fiery Gizzard Trail, Tracy City, 10–11

Great Smoky Mountains National Park, Gatlinburg, 63–66

Land Between the Lakes, Dover, 124

Obed National Wild and Scenic River, Wartburg, 50

Radnor Lake State Natural Area, Nashville, 106

Red Clay State Historic Area, Cleveland, 74

Reelfoot Lake, Tiptonville, 129–132

Reflection Riding, Chattanooga, 19–20

Savage Gulf State Natural Area, Beersheba Springs, 10, 14

Sewanee Natural Bridge State Natural Area, Sewanee, 6–8

South Cumberland State Park, Tracy City, 10–11